The Voice Inside

Going From Lost to Found

BY

JOCELYN WREEDE

THE VOICE INSIDE

Ordering Information: Special discounts are available on quantity purchases by corporations, associations, as well as U.S. trade bookstores and wholesalers.

DREAMSTARTERS

www.DreamStartersPublishing.com

Table of Contents

Dedication 4

Foreword 12

Introduction.. 14

Adversity Equals Fuel.. 17

From Dark to Light.. 34

Rebirth and Reinvention.. 48

I Am Called 65

Life's Cycles 84

Balls To the Wall.. 115

Find Your People and Your Purpose 127

The Mess of It.. 143

Conclusion... 152

Contact Page 155

Dedication

I dedicate this book to my sweet, sweet Gavin. You are the reason I've always wanted to do better, to BE better.

You are the reason for everything I do. I want you to know and recognize what healthy relationships and people look like. How to respect and love yourself enough to not let anyone's opinions dictate your drive and success in life. I want you to reach for the stars!

The day you were born, after 5½ hours of pushing and pain, with the doctors' attempts and with all the devices at their disposal, and finally a c-section to bring you into this world. Your dad put you cheek to cheek with me. While they stitched me up, with tears running down my cheeks, my first words to you out of the womb were "you're my greatest accomplishment."

I am so proud of the man you are becoming! Your empathetic heart for others, your sweet caring demeanor, and your mama's grit for not letting anyone walk on you are just a few things I'm most proud of. The number one thing though, is your love for God. Wanting to please your Father in Heaven by being a servant.

Anytime you've seen a homeless person, a suffering animal, or even a piece of trash on the ground, you immediately want to help. You've had us give money or resources to others when we didn't even think we had them to give. Your pure heart and empathy are fine qualities that will get you far in life.

Our man-child, you are going to have such a great head start in your life from the things we've exposed you to as well as the things we've deliberately not exposed you to.

We have strong moral convictions and core values in this family, we set healthy boundaries, when they are stomped on that's a non-negotiable for us. We don't entertain toxic people or relationships that go against everything we stand for.

Most will never learn the things you're learning as a child. To keep your inner sanctum healthy, supportive, and free from drama, lies, and manipulation. We are so excited to see where your life takes you free from all the poison that so many just settle for in a mediocre life. You know at a young age what you're worth and what you deserve.

We love you "Boogie Woogie," more than you'll ever know this side of Heaven. I dedicate this Life's work, this passion, and God's call, to YOU. Without you, I would have never had the courage or the desire to WANT to be and do better. "You're my greatest accomplishment." Thank you.

More Thank You's...

THE VOICE INSIDE

There are so many people to thank in 49 years of life, and I will no doubt forget many who have molded and shaped me into being the person able to break free from the mindsets and indoctrinations placed on us all by societal standards and generational cycles. First though, I want to thank My Father in Heaven, without his relentless pursuit of me through all of my pitfalls, sins, and defiance, His love for me never wavered.

The passion He put in me along with the calling on my life to help other abuse survivors, those still being abused, to help put an end to unhealthy generational cycles, to shine a light on psychological abuse, to be the truth teller, and so much more is such a blessing to me, and at times has felt like a curse. I know it's all His will to bring awareness to the dark places people tend to ignore and deny, or to hate on others rather than explore His truth, so I accepted this tough, tough ask knowing HE will always walk beside me.

I thank my mother for doing the best she could with the know how she had, I still pray daily for her hurts and internal demons to be squashed, and for her to walk into complete healing with a mindset that lets her know she IS enough, that she is loved, to know what she deserves, and how to obtain it all moving into healthy relationships, and a growth mindset instead of a victim one.

I thank my biological father for his lack of love and abandonment because without that I wouldn't have the grit or strength I have today.

http://jocelynwreede.com/

I thank my baby sister; she changed all of our lives for the better coming into this world. She's my constant ride-or-die. Our relationship is so precious to me, I'll always be there for her no matter what.

Thank you to my guys, they're my stronghold. My shelter in which I build on God's foundation. My husband, as you'll read in this book, is the absolute strongest man I know. When he was near death, he showed me what life is truly about. What we deserve and to go after everything we want in life; now, not later.

Thank you to Brenda Sanford, founder of Light the Way Christian Counseling, she was the pivotal mentor/therapist who helped begin the transformation in me. We talked about this book in many sessions together ten years or more ago. She is fabulous as both a professional and a friend, and I'm so blessed to have been under her mentorship and guidance for so many years. She led me to Celebrate Recovery and to Pastors Matt Sandlin and Shelly Stevenson, who also were steppingstones on my healing journey. She is just a top-notch individual, and I love her dearly.

Thank you to Bonnie Weiss, Founder of The Center for Christian Coaching, along with Susan Underwood who taught, mentored, and prayed with and for me as well. Bonnie's story, Christian Life Coaching course, and absolute anointing helped grow my mind and heart tenfold. She has a way about her that can only be Christ given; she just radiates love. Susan was hand selected by Bonnie to join her team after having taken the course too, and she must have seen herself in Susan because she too illuminates all the God given traits of an exceptional human and teacher. These two women along with all the women in my class, I will forever cherish as steppingstones into helping me to accept God's call on my life as well as being the beautiful women they all are inside and out.

Thank you to my Stepchildren, ya kept me on my toes! I wanted to be a safe place for you to fall, to help you without overstepping, and to love you as my own. You didn't make that easy, but I thank you because the trials helped open our eyes to the fact we weren't surrounding ourselves or you with the right people. "We don't know what we don't know." Once we knew, we chose to exemplify strength to you, so you could find your own ways out of the darkness with a glimmer of light from us. We'll never stop praying for your complete healing and for the strength to face all your truths. To weather that storm head-on, and come out as victorious and with the mindset and heart strong in knowledge and faith as we were able to do. Break those cycles. We're so proud of you both and your individual progress of exploring, recognizing, putting the messy pieces of your lives together slowly, to finally know the truths that have eluded you for so many years that made you hurt and angry. Like they say, nothing worth it is easy, and personal development, mindset growth, and healing are the hardest parts we face in life if we're brave enough to go on that journey, but it's also the most freeing and rewarding outside of one's personal relationship with Christ. Spread your wings and fly, never give up on chasing who HE designed you to be, keep pressing.

Thank you to all of our precious grandbabies; they all bring us such joy. They're all so unique in their own ways and bring huge smiles to our hearts with each of their little personalities. We treasure our time with them so much. We've often said they are like God's gift to us, to make up for what was stolen from us for so many years by several (that you'll read about in the book). Our love for those children could never be explained in words.

Thank you to all of my incredible coaches and mentors. There are many. First, I want to thank Keaton and Limitless Society. This is the group that literally changed the trajectory of everything. The one that took everything I had already learned with previous coaches and therapists and put the pieces together for me. Keaton graciously agreed to write the foreword for this book, which is such a blessing to me, and I know God put him in my path. I look forward to our growing friendship in the future as I became a lifetime member of his group. I had been trying to decide about a new coaching group, and I felt a pull to Keaton. We chatted a few times, so eventually I jumped in scared as hell, but I did. The cost of Keaton's group was the exact combined cost of the two groups I was leaving to join limitless. God confirming it in that way was comforting to me, as I had been with my other coaches for over a year. I learned a lot from those two coaches, I just felt like it was time to move on and reach for something more. So, I also thank Sandy Krakowski/A real Change, and Jennifer Alwood/The Better Way Program for teaching me about stocks/trading and online business, as well as being vessels for God in spreading his word.

Thank you to all of my other groups and all of the healthy friends I've made in those groups. They are literally part of my daily go-to routine now and I appreciate so much knowing there are people who have my back and to be able to bounce things off of, to pray for me, and just to BE THERE for whatever for one another. Aside from Limitless, my other groups are Victorious with Nick Santonastaso, 801 Collective that my friend Thomas Cobb started, The Young Entrepreneurs Syndicate with Jim Riley, Rod Kuntz, and Rachel Svoboda, Mike's Inner Circle, with Mike Fallat, also the publisher of this book, and most recently Rogue World, with Dusky Dalton & Todd Bezates. Last but definitely not least my health and fitness coaches in the Fit Life Tribe program, Trista Harrison and Marisa Pace, I met Trista in Limitless and joined her program. They all bring tons of wisdom and knowledge. The best thing I've ever done for myself is getting coaches. I will never regret going all-in on ME. We're just getting started, with the help and guidance of all of these coaches and the people inside them we are unstoppable. This book is just the beginning as to what's to come.

Finally, I want to thank ALL my haters from over the course of my entire life. Aside from God, you were the driving force that fueled me. So, what was meant to destroy and break me had the opposite effect. You built me. So, I thank you. Without your evil ways, unwillingness to be honest, unwillingness to humble yourselves, unwillingness to repent and change, unwillingness to learn and grow, to heal your own inner child, I wouldn't have the strong mind I have today, or be the pillar of strength to keep getting back up in the face of adversity, unkindness, and trauma. Thank you from the bottom of my heart for doubting me and providing me with my most admired qualities.

Foreword

My name is Keaton Hoskins but many know me as "The Muscle" from the Diesel brothers television show. I am a business entrepreneur. I own and run a coaching group called Limitless Society that is meant to help people become their best selves. I also own a nutrition supplement company (1 Mission Nutrition), along with partial ownership to Dirty Dough and Fitcon. I travel regularly and speak at events. I am a father of soon to be 5 little girls and have the most amazing wife a man could ask for.

Me and Jocelyn connected through Limitless Society. She has been in the group almost as long as the group has been around. She is such an amazing individual and stepped out in faith to go all in on herself. She has not only gotten on almost every group call but she implements so much of the tools and advice given to her. Her growth and participation and constant desire to help others is beyond impressive. She is also massively talented in so many areas and more than willing to help others in their business and in their personal lives. She also makes some killer syrup (order yourself some).

I believe this book can and will inspire many to get out of their "rut". Change is hard and so many people do not want to do the work it takes to make the needed changes in their lives for success and happiness. This book is created by someone who has done the work and can truly help. Especially for those who are having a hard time finding their why and their direction. Jocelyn wasn't given those tools like so many of us aren't but she took what she was given, what she was taught, the example she had and she broke free from it and became the one in her family to make that generational change. You can see from those she has in her life how her choices have helped and affected them. She truly has done the work to become, as Ed Mylett puts it, "the one".

I chose to write this forward for Jocelyn because I believe in her. I believe in her efforts, in her desire, and in her as a person. I can't wait to see what you do next Jocelyn and to see what your family does next because of your present example. You are a divine daughter of God and he has great plans for you and those you help and serve.

Keaton Hoskins

Introduction

Like so many people, I experienced a childhood that was more along the lines of the "evil stepparent" trope, except the stepparent in question happened to be my mother's second husband.

A few years after my real father abandoned our family, leaving my mother a single mom to me and my younger sister, my mom remarried. My new "father" would prove to have a dark side that he somehow managed to keep hidden from my mother for several years. During that time, I took it upon myself to become my sister's protector. After all, I was the stronger and fiercer one of the two of us. Sometimes I prevailed, and sometimes I didn't. My mother, sister, and I did eventually exit my stepfather's life, but his cruelty had already cast a long, dark shadow over my sister and my formative years.

All trauma is awful and consuming, leaving lifelong physical and emotional scars, but childhood abuse, in any form, can prevent certain regions of the brain from ever developing properly. It is not surprising that survivors of child abuse not only run the risk of specific physical health problems but are more likely to suffer emotional and psychological problems, such as depression, low self-esteem, and the inability to maintain positive relationships. The only way to escape those damaging effects is to seek help and guidance, which is much easier said than done. I know that for a fact because that was the case with me.

I tried to maintain a tough exterior while my stepfather wielded his power—after all, I was my sister's protector, a leader, and a star athlete —but going forward, there was no way to keep the spiritual and emotional underpinnings of abuse from affecting everything in my life. Under the weight of my childhood trauma, I turned to the numbing embrace of alcohol.

During that time, I met and married my first husband. The relationship ended after several tumultuous years. As our relationship deteriorated, I sank into the darkest depression of my life and nearly lost all the fight in me. Miraculously—and I don't use that word lightly—just when I imagined there was nowhere left to turn, I had a life-altering encounter ... with the man who I knew to be my soul mate and later my second husband. I believe this was no accident, but rather a divine intervention.

With the emotional support of my second husband, I was able to embark on a path of self-discovery, determined to understand the events of my past, break the cycle of abuse, and find purpose in my life. Along my journey—and through another miracle—Jesus Himself, urging me to embrace my true identity and become an inspiration for others, joined me.

THE VOICE INSIDE

From the shadows of childhood abuse, to escape into alcoholism, to prolonged bouts of anxiety and deep despair and, finally, redemption, I believe that my story illustrates the resilient spirit of the human soul and the transformative power of divine intervention. It proves that life is a journey filled with twists, turns, and unexpected detours, countless challenges, failures, and times of complete chaos. However, amidst the chaos lies a profound truth: *the mess often equals the message.* In other words, our most significant moments of personal growth often arise from the challenges we face.

I found my way out of darkness and into a future lit by love, personal success, and the power of Jesus. I believe my story to be a testament of healing, redemption, and the importance of self-discovery, which I hope will inspire everyone seeking the same.

Like the barn on the cover of this book was lost to decay and neglect only to be found once again through restoration, people, too, can experience a restoration of their spirit. I know because I am one of six generations of women who have either owned and/or lived on this farm. This barn has withstood generations and represents God's constant presence. He also gave me the subtitle of this book 10 years ago.

Chapter 1

Adversity Equals Fuel

"Every adversity, every failure, every heartache carries with it the seed of an equal or greater benefit."

Napoleon Hill

One of the first Bible stories I remember hearing was the story of David and Goliath. To an impressionable six-year-old, the story of a child named David, who was braver than all the adults around him, was prophetic.

THE VOICE INSIDE

"One day, a warrior named Goliath challenged the people of Israel to send someone to fight him. Everyone was scared, but David stepped forward because he believed God would give him strength. David faced the giant, towering Goliath with only his sling and stone. He aimed his sling and hit Goliath right in the forehead. Goliath fell to the ground, defeated. David's faith in God gave him the courage to overcome the kind of adversity that seemed impossible to all the skeptical adults around him."

As a child, I couldn't believe there was a Bible story about someone not unlike myself. It immediately grabbed a special place in my heart. At the time, even though I was only six years old, I thought, *I am just like David.* At church, I often heard of this story, *"Now, when you have a child, you can tell them the story of David and Goliath."*

By the grace of God, I did have that opportunity nearly thirty years later.

I read the story to my young son because I wanted him to know early on that,

"When we feel small or face overwhelming challenges, we can find strength within ourselves and trust in something greater to help us overcome those challenges."

JOCELYN WREEDE

Recently, a friend asked me why I thought God had given her so many challenges in her life.

"Why should I have to jump through so many hoops to get what I want?" she asked.

I reminded her of how adversity fueled David. I explained that adversity in one's life is the most significant motivators for change, and that God was telling her to closely examine the reason for her challenges and to trust that if she made the effort required of her, she would find guidance.

I know a thing or two about adversity because it was never a stranger to me. From a young age, dysfunction and abuse were all around me. However, I knew instinctively, even as a child, that I would find a way to be better than the people around me and that, when I grew up, I would never treat people as I was treated. *There's more for you out there*, I remember telling myself. *You're going to do great things.*

"Consider it all joy, my brethren, when you encounter various trials, knowing that the testing of your faith produces endurance. And let endurance have its perfect result, so that you may be perfect and complete, lacking in nothing."

James 1:2-4 NKJV

http://jocelynwreede.com/

In The Beginning

I was five when my father' had an affair with my mother's best friend. Not surprisingly, my parents divorced soon after. Looking back, I think it wrecked my mother, but I had no way of knowing what she felt then. Unbeknownst to me, she had her own problems to deal with—remnants of a life before I even came into the picture.

My mother was a strong woman who did everything in her power to try to do her best for herself and her daughters. She worked full-time for the Farm Service Agency—part of the federal government—in Bellefontaine, Ohio. Although she ensured my sister and I never wanted for the essentials, we still knew things could be better.

After my father left, my sister and I were shuttled back and forth from my mother's home—what I considered my real home—and my father's place, but it was more out of a sense of obligation that my father even agreed to spend time with us. At seventeen months younger than me, my sister wasn't quite old enough to be aware of my father's indifference, but I was. It didn't take me long to realize that Dad didn't give a shit about anyone but himself. His weekend visits became increasingly less frequent. At some point, he even stopped making child support payments.

Unfortunately, in the early 1980s, women had little recourse when their deadbeat exes were behind in child support. The courts didn't bother to take any action against them, my father included. The government didn't take money from my dad's checks or confiscate his driver's license as they would today, so my mother was left holding the proverbial financial bag.

Fortunately, my mother worked a steady job. She maintained house payments, but any "extras" were out of reach. I will forever have the image of her hunched over the kitchen table, poring over past due bills, holding her head, cursing my dad, and crying. Dad owed her thousands of dollars, and she could hold nothing over his head to make him liable. Not even suing him in court changed anything. He responded by signing over his parental rights so he wouldn't have to pay. And just like that, he was free and clear of all his financial, familial, emotional, and otherwise responsibilities. Any anger and resentment I had was squirreled away, hidden, and ignored. As far as my mother was concerned it was good riddance.

I realize now that she needed to take that stance to persevere and care for her daughters. However, it was difficult for me to adopt the same attitude as a child. It would be years before I could process the damage my father had inflicted and my deep sense of abandonment. In the meantime, I instinctively felt I had to step into my new role as a surrogate parent to my younger sister. I didn't have a choice in the matter, or at least I didn't think I had a choice. It was just the three of us … until my mother met husband number two.

Patterns of Abuse

My mother wouldn't make the same mistake again by marrying someone who couldn't take on the financial responsibilities of a family. The man who would become our new daddy may have been a solid breadwinner. Unfortunately, he was also dealing with his own demons— demons that could turn him from Dr. Jekyll to Mr. Hyde. Before he even married my mother, it was crystal clear that he was as equally unfit to be a parent as my biological father.

I must have been about ten years old the night he, my mother, my sister, and I were sitting around the kitchen table when he backhanded me, knocking me clear off my chair. To this day, I don't remember what I could have said that would have been so terrible to cause a grown man to haul off and bloody a child's face. My mom was in tears, and she yelled at him to stop. Looking back, I think mom was doing the best she could with what she had after a lifetime of unhealthy family relationships and denial. How would she even know a good man if she saw one?

Although he never abused my mother, my new dad was a mean alcoholic when it came to my sister and I. He came home from work at 3:07 p.m. every day, a couple of hours before my mom. The first thing he would do was crack open his first Old Milwaukee beer. Then he would have another and another until he was drunk and angry, just drunk and passed out, or until he went to bed at eleven p.m. My sister and I never knew which it would be or when he would turn his indiscriminate anger on us.

My stepfather's house rules were strict. One of his rules was that my sister and I weren't allowed to watch TV after school, or have a snack, even though we were famished by the time we got home. Of course, being kids, we ignored the rules. We would grab some food and settle in front of the TV. If we happened to be eating when he got home, we would hide our plates under the sofa. If we were watching TV, we'd have to remember to turn it off with enough time for it to cool off before he could lay his hand on it. If the TV were warm, he would know we had been watching it, in defiance of his rules. And when that happened, he would beat the shit out of us. Almost always with a board he had.

My sister wound up getting the worst of the beatings, mostly because I fought back with vengeance, and she didn't. I always tried to protect her, but it was oftentimes useless.

We had two hours in the house with our stepdad daily before our mom came home. He would grab a two-by-four and use it on my sister, leaving welts all over her body. Sometimes I could hold him off by dragging my sister into a closet and hiding. During times like that, we clung to the protection offered in Psalms 56:11: "In God I have put my trust: I will not be afraid, what man can do unto me." That verse protected us for many years. It is still my shelter.

Sometimes he would grow too weary or drunk to get off his chair, and we'd be safe. Like clockwork, the beatings and abuse would stop at precisely 5:30 p.m. when my mother walked through the door.

On weekends, my stepdad managed to be on his best behavior, so my mother never actually witnessed most of the beatings. It would be hard to imagine that she was unaware of the psychological abuse, but she was under the strain of those threats, too. My sister and I kept our mouths shut. Something told us that our mother might be unable to handle knowing the truth, but that didn't stop my growing rage.

One night, I reached a breaking point. My mother was home, in the kitchen, cleaning up after dinner, while my stepdad sat drunk in his favorite chair. I grabbed a baseball bat and went into the living room, where I stood over him. I heard my sister call to my mother, panicked, she then yelled, "Jocelyn!" A minute later, my mom was beside me, prying the bat from my tightly clenched fists. She stopped me then, but I'm sure I would have started swinging if she hadn't. And I don't know when I would have stopped. Or if.

For a long time, I wondered, *Why is this happening to me? Why would He let this happen?* I sometimes went to church with my mom or grandparents and prayed to God to make it stop. *Please make it stop.* But it didn't. Since God didn't seem to be listening, I made a promise to myself that, one day, I was going to be the most amazing parent, the best friend, the best wife, and the best human. I would show God that I didn't need His help, anyway, and that I would manage on my own. I had no way of knowing then that He was listening to me the whole time and writing my story with all of it.

It should go without saying that I would never choose to repeat those years, but what I can say about them is that they served to build the core of the woman I would become, of the believer, the fierce protector, and spiritual counselor I would grow to be. It would help me to withstand abuse and triumph over obstacles in my life. But first, it would drive me down a long road of self-destruction.

Following Trauma

After nearly seven years of abuse and beatings, my mother finally came to see and accept what was going on and took action against my stepdad. He ended up in a court-ordered detox center. While he was there, my mother took the opportunity to pack up our house and move us out.

Ironically, my stepdad was like a different person when he got out of detox, so much so that he helped us move into our own little place. It's funny. My mother never actually "turned" on my stepdad. He had been "a good provider," which meant that, unlike my real dad, he held down a steady job and helped pay the bills. As a kid, I couldn't wrap my brain around her defense of him. I still can't, as a mother myself. However, after he came out of a long stint in rehab, sober and somewhat repentant, I did see that his Mr. Hyde personality could mostly be attributed to alcohol abuse. Which of course is still no excuse for abuse, or the lifelong damaging effects it leaves. My mother was somehow able to see past the negative. I came to the conclusion that my mother was either decidedly optimistic about people—men in particular—or her inability to see what was happening had more to do with her own perceived lack of self-worth. I now know it was the latter having watched the same abusive cycles repeat in relationships since.

Somewhere between my mother's second and third marriage, we all moved into my mother's then boyfriend's house. Even though he was a decent enough man, the trauma my sister and I had experienced had already settled deep in the core of our beings. I was a high school freshman, and my sister was in the eighth grade when a manifestation of that trauma became apparent.

My sister stayed home from school, feigning sickness, after my mother and I left for the day. Alone in the house, my sister slit her wrists. Somehow, she had the wherewithal to call Mom, so Mom could call a neighbor to the house and get an ambulance there in time to save my sister's life. My sister survived but remained in the children's psychiatric ward under a suicide watch for weeks. Unfortunately, she would make several attempts at suicide over the course of several years. She was eventually diagnosed as manic depressive, which today we know as bi-polar. She would go on to repeat the same unhealthy cycles my mom did in her relationships, with abusive type individuals. Cycles.

During that time, I remember being at school, sitting in class, and breaking down. That was so unlike me. I was the resilient one, the one who was never rattled, at least not outwardly.

My teacher took me out of class and sat in the cafeteria with me watching me sob. I sat there for a while until I finally stopped crying.

Not long afterward, the counselor at the hospital where my sister had been placed spoke some very important words of wisdom I had not heard until then. She said, "You can hold all that junk inside you as long as possible. You can keep up the tough act and pretend that you're okay, but it will manifest eventually, whether you want it to or not." I heard her words but didn't have the wisdom to heed them. At least, not yet.

It would be a long road for me to understand how childhood trauma and abuse influenced my sense of self and forced me to make harmful decisions. The real tragedy is that once we adjust to abuse, we are at risk of considering abuse our normal and acceptable condition. Like my mom and sister had. I didn't want that to be my normal and was determined for it not to be.

Through my own research and my voracious appetite for reading and seeking answers, I would also realize that my trauma was due not only to my stepdad but also to the father who had abandoned us. Not only that, but also my mother was completely unprepared to care for us in such an environment. She did not understand that she, herself, needed proper healing in order to not attract abusive type men.

I had spent nearly seven formative years walking on eggshells daily, trying to defend my sister and myself. I thought I was okay, but I wasn't.

For a long while, I would suffer the effects of my childhood in my adult relationships. Somehow, though, I would eventually find the will and the spirit to seek help from a greater source. Until then, I would have a lot of painful lessons to learn.

A Psychic Band-Aid

It wasn't long before I turned to smoking and drinking heavily. I had been an athlete throughout my days in junior high and much of high school, mostly summer ball — determined and fit—but all I wanted to do now was escape and be the party girl. Party, party, party. That became my war cry. As the counselor at the hospital had predicted, I was under my own misguided opinion that I was okay. But really, all I was doing was numbing myself from the pain I had experienced and didn't know what to do with it. I wasn't ready to thoroughly examine "the junk inside." Instead, I put a Band-Aid on the open wound that had become my life.

Not surprisingly, I suffered my first panic attack when I was eighteen and would continue to suffer from them for the next two decades. For nearly two years after that first attack, I holed up in my house with severe agoraphobia, afraid to venture past my front door. When I finally conquered my agoraphobia, I was about twenty years old.

The following few years were like an alcohol and cigarette-stoked blur. I couldn't even say where I was or who I was with most of the time, but eventually, at the ripe old age of twenty-five, I came to long enough to get married. Perhaps I subconsciously hoped the marriage would save me from spiraling further, but if the party had raged before I had married, it showed no signs of slowing afterward.

There is so much I wish I could forget about my first marriage, but again, like the events of my childhood, it would become a driving force in making me the person I am today.

I met my husband at sixteen when we worked together at KFC, running around, drinking and partying after work with friends. Many of us had married young, so we weren't near ready to curtail our partying, and marriage didn't do anything to stop any of us from sleeping around. We were all drinking as hard as we had in our teens, most nights and weekends. It took me a while to realize that, like everyone else, I was trying to fill some void in my life. But, unlike my friends, the partying only made me feel worse. I was just running on a hamster wheel and numbing myself day after day.

I woke up one day with the realization that I would never feel any peace or contentment if I kept up that lifestyle. However, that didn't mean I left the marriage. That never occurred to me as a solution, but I did start to pull back from partying.

Since high school, I enjoyed reading psychology books because I had always been interested in why people did what they did, so I returned to those books. I told my husband I was done partying and bar hopping, wanting to spend time alone, without my husband or my "so-called friends & family". Though, not yet at a point where I was seeking help, I felt like I was at least treating myself better.

Unfortunately, I had no support system in place, so my isolation started to take a toll on my psyche. I was trying to take care of myself, but all my time alone distanced me from people in my life. My husband and I were spending more and more time apart. When we were together, he was mean and distant, as though he was harboring a secret. My only response was a degree of paranoia, which led me to play detective. I started searching through my husband's pockets and wallet when he was in the shower.

I knew in my heart that the marriage was doomed. I was burdened by my own load of troubles. My husband's emotional distance was the straw that broke the camel's back. I had cheated on him during all of the partying. Ironically, when I searched his pockets and found the receipts for lavish dinners and tickets, I realized his infidelity. Even though I had been honest with him, he had withheld the truth from me.

I had seen it coming, but I was still devastated. I could hear a faint voice from within telling me that I was at a crucial turning point. It said that divorce would eventually be the best for me. I would have the opportunity to build myself back better and stronger. The voice was faint, but it reminded me of going to church with my mom or grandparents, where I would repeatedly hear that Jesus loved me.

I remembered one verse in particular:

"As the Father loved me, I too have loved you. Remain in my love. If you keep my commandments, you will remain in my love, just as I kept my Father's commandments and remain in His love. I have said these things to you so that My joy will be in you and your joy will be complete."

John 15:9-17 CEB

I knew I needed to heal, but I wasn't sure how to do it. I had no course, no game plan. For whatever reason, I was still turning a deaf ear to the higher voice in my head. I didn't think it possible, but I had even farther to fall before I could begin my higher journey. What would it take to navigate out of the storm that had become my life?

Takeaway

- Look at adversity as fuel, building character and laying down the strengths you can use in your life.
- God hears you when you pray to Him, even if His answer is not immediate.

- Abuse can be subtle or obvious, but it is insidious. If you do not have a sense of your own worth, you will never recognize the abuse in your life.
- Childhood trauma and abuse will follow you and affect every area of your life until you take the time to look within.
- There is no quick fix to psychological and spiritual healing. Undoubtedly, sex, drugs, and alcohol are the easiest ways to put a Band-Aid on an open emotional wound, but the fix won't last. In fact, it only makes things worse.

Chapter 2

From Dark to Light

"And once the storm is over, you won't remember how you made it through, how you managed to survive. You won't even be sure whether the storm is really over. But one thing is certain. When you come out of the storm, you won't be the same person who walked in. That's what this storm's all about."

Haruki Murakami

The day after I found out my husband was cheating on me, he went to work as usual. While he was gone, I packed his belongings in trash bags and threw the bags onto the lawn.

When my husband arrived home, he picked up the bags and left, leaving me alone with all our bills.

I felt like I had nowhere to go, no one to turn to. To keep up with expenses, I found two jobs. During the day, I groomed dogs. At night, I delivered pizza, day in and day out. I didn't see friends, and I didn't see family. I just worked and worked, coming home to an empty house, exhausted and emotionally depleted. I was on autopilot and losing altitude.

Looking back on that time, I can see that I was being engulfed by depression, but all I heard from the people around me was that I would get over "it" eventually—*My failed marriage? My depression? My loss of hope?* —and that I was just feeling "down." A friend suggested that I was simply sad, and sooner or later, I would cease to be sad. But depression is not just a feeling of sadness. It's a persistent state. Not only did I not have the tools to climb out of that state, but I also felt there was no reason to try.

Sometimes I just came home and curled into the fetal position and cried. Sometimes I could barely bring myself to change out of my clothes before passing out, and then, when I woke in the morning, I had to drag myself out of bed. Fortunately, I didn't have any important decisions to make when I was grooming dogs or delivering pizza, because I couldn't concentrate on anything other than my misery. Whenever I could manage to do so, I would write about how I was feeling to try to exorcise all those bad thoughts from my head, but it didn't help. I wasn't able to dig myself out of my psychological hole—at least not alone. Instead, the hole only deepened.

The Crash

Within two weeks my husband left, my dog of twelve years disappeared, and my grandfather passed away. Before he passed, I went to the nursing home where he was living and sat with him. I held his hand in those final hours before he passed, as my sister stood, bawling over him.

Calmly, I said to him, *"You can go. We'll all be fine. You don't have to worry about any of us. You go. There's a pretty little lady waiting for you on the other side. You go to her."*

He opened his eyes for the first time since the night before and looked right at me. He squeezed my hand ever so slightly before taking his last breath.

I was so glad I was there for him. Years later, I would find myself in the same position with my other grandfather, holding his right hand, telling him he could go and be with Jesus, sure by then that God had placed me beside both men to ease their passing. That first time, I strongly felt that I had to be with my grandfather, holding his hand when he transitioned, though I didn't know why. I wondered, Is *there some other force at work?*

I didn't have the time or the wherewithal to dive deep into answers because I had to get back to my work grind—a grind that was becoming unsustainable. I was so stressed that I wasn't even eating. At one point, there was only a box of Ho Ho's in the house and a six-pack of Bud Light that only stayed cold because I kept it outside in the snow. My electricity was shut off.

Despite my efforts, I couldn't keep up with the bills. Eventually, my gas was also shut off. I had to run a small space heater in my bedroom so I wouldn't freeze to death in my sleep. It was the dead of an Ohio winter, and I was living in the one room in the house that wasn't freezing. I would get home, shut my bedroom door, power up the heater, and try to sleep before I had to be at work.

One night, I bought a bottle of Jack Daniels on the way home, to keep warm, to drown my sorrow, to forget. I didn't even drink hard liquor, but I drank nearly the whole bottle. Afterward, I stumbled from room to room until I came upon one of my grandfather's old shotguns. I don't know why any of his guns were left in the house. My family should have removed them all when they cleaned out his belongings. But not only was one still there, it was loaded. I grabbed it and brought it into the living room; shotgun in one hand, the near-empty bottle of Jack in the other. I was ready to end it all in a brilliant, dramatic fashion.

I took a bullet out of the weapon. Then, with a pen knife, I carved the name of my ex-husband: "Mike." in it. Sobbing, drunk, I loaded it back in the gun and pressed the muzzle underneath my chin. I even took the safety off and had my finger on the trigger gently squeezing. On second thought, I put the gun down momentarily and tried to call my ex. He was staying with a married couple I knew. The wife answered the phone. I can't remember what I said to her, but I can only imagine how out of my mind I must have sounded. She also thought so because she immediately called my sister, who then called my mom.

Before I knew it, my mother was beating down my front door, hysterically. I want to say that she took me in her arms and hugged me, but that wasn't the case. She grabbed the gun, and the Jack Daniels then batted me around, screaming through her tears, *"What are you thinking? Are you crazy?"* She was a fit to be tied and, quite literally, trying to knock sense back into me. She sobered me up then took stock of the house. It was as cold inside as outside. No heat, no electricity, no groceries, and a stack of unpaid bills on the dining room table.

"Get your things. I'm taking you to your sister's house!" she screamed. "That's it. I don't want to hear another word on the

subject. You're going to stay with her whether you like it or not."

I was in no position to argue. My mother saved me, but for the life of me, I didn't know how or why at the time. I knew she loved me, but I needed more than her love. I needed answers. I tried praying, *why was my life prolonged when I am in so much pain? Why?* I waited for an answer, for some direction, but I got nothing.

Years later, after much counseling and soul searching, I realized that the abused child in me hadn't had the chance to air her grievances and mourn her childhood. The message I had been living with since early childhood was that I was not good enough to be loved. Surely, I wasn't good enough for my father to want to stay with me. I wasn't good enough to be protected. For years, I told myself that if I had been a better kid, none of the terrible things in my life would have happened. If I had been "good," I wouldn't be such a mess, and my mother wouldn't be dragging me to my sister's house.

Grace Happens

My sister didn't want me living with her any more than I wanted to be there. As much as I was her protector when we were kids, we fought like cats and dogs. She resented my presence but couldn't say no to our mother. Instead, she gave me laundry lists of things to do around the house, as though I were a live-in maid. She didn't care that I was working two jobs. She wasn't interested in my misery, and I wasn't doing anything to quell it.

Instead of picking up any pieces left of my life, I tried to break it up even more. I started drinking at my pizza delivery job. After my shift was over, I would drive a hundred miles an hour, sheets to the wind, to the local bar my ex and I frequented and continue drinking. When last call was over, I would drive to my sister's house, crawl up the stairs, and into bed. Night after night, work, drink, sleep...lather, rinse, and repeat. By the grace of God, I made it home each night without dying or killing anyone else in my drunken state.

I was utterly numbing myself to distract myself from my life and unbearable pain. My stressful living situation, menial jobs, failed marriage, unhealthy relationships, and feelings of worthlessness, I didn't want clarity about any of those things because I knew it would only bring me more pain.

One Tuesday night, I walked into the bar and sat next to my friend Jim, who I often sat with. Jim and I had gone to high school together, and that night, he was there with a good friend of his, Adam, who had also gone to school with us. They were sitting with a seat between them.

I walked up and kidded, *"Oh, you guys saved a seat for me?"*

They both answered, *"Yes,"* so I settled in between them, and we talked.

Adam said he'd seen me in the bar with my ex and had wondered why we were always apart. It was funny that he'd noticed, but it was true. Whenever I came in with my ex, he would make a beeline to the back of the bar to play pool, and I would stay in the front, talking to people and accepting drinks from anyone who would buy them for me.

Jim didn't say much that night, but he did look pleased that Adam and I were getting on so well.

Jim was a sweetheart. We think he purposely set us up that night because Adam said he would never have come out on a Tuesday if Jim hadn't insisted, which he had.

Jim had joined up with an annual drinking excursion—a tradition where people hopped around the lake drinking at local bars. Adam and I decided to stay home, but we told Jim to call us, no matter the time, so we could pick him up.

By nine that night we hadn't heard from Jim, so we started calling him. He never answered. We learned that he had missed a curve driving home and driven straight into a tree.

Jim's death tore Adam apart and rocked me to my core. Just a week earlier, during one of our nights drinking together, Jim told me he admired Adam's love for his two kids from a previous marriage. He had shared with me all the things he wanted out of life—including a family and kids of his own—and then, a week later, he was gone. By then, Adam and I had fallen in love. We would go on to name our son Gavin *"James"* after Jim.

Out of the Void

I felt as though Adam was my knight in shining armor. He was sweet, considerate, and strong—the type of person I'd been searching for most of my adult life. It was as if my darkest days had set me up for what I most needed. As if I had finally gained more clarity and had somehow drawn Adam into my life, though I would come to believe that a higher power had been doing the driving all along. Author and motivational speaker, Willie Jolly, said it best in the title of his 1999 book, A *Setback is a Setup for a Comeback.*

It was as though Adam represented the beginning of my comeback. Until we had met, I had been numbing myself, trying to escape my life. I can easily say that I was drunk for the entirety of my twenties, which only exacerbated my panic attacks. Finally, at thirty, I realized that the vices I had accumulated—the drinking, marajuana at different times, the sleeping around and, most importantly, my disregard for my own life—were filling the void I had fallen into. Every dark and dangerous thing that had happened to me helped me move the compass and point it toward Adam.

Committing to Adam was easy, but I thought giving up drinking would be nearly impossible. After all, everyone I knew drank. Drinking has been touted through the ages as the most natural social thing. When I was in a beer haze, I could talk to anyone at any time, but was I really communicating with anyone? I don't think so. It felt more pleasant to dull my senses than to allow them access to the people and places around me.

Deep down inside, I knew I was drinking to mask my sadness, isolation, and disappointment with the world. I felt sorry for myself, and drinking gave me a pass. I drank to keep my emotional skeletons in the closet and to prevent myself from facing my demons head-on. I knew I couldn't keep on the way I was going because it would ultimately destroy me and everyone I loved.

There is Always a Darker Place

It would be several more years before I realized that finding my husband and giving up drinking was only the beginning of my journey out of the dark and into the light. I had always had an inkling of a power greater than anything in this physical world. Hadn't I imagined, at six years old, that I would find a way to be better than the people around me? Hadn't I told myself that I was going to do important things?

THE VOICE INSIDE

I'll never forget a phone call I had with a friend while living in my grandparents house. I was sobbing about my marriage and how I didn't think my life could get any worse.

He told me,

"Jocelyn, I know you think you've hit rock bottom, but you can always go deeper. There's always a deeper place to sink into, so you can stay on your path downward or move in the other direction. You can choose to go in the other direction."

It took a while before I finally went in that other direction and started to examine the mess, I'd been in. I realized that not only had I run the risk of drinking myself to death or killing myself on the road, but I had also run the risk of killing someone else. It was, quite literally, a sobering reality, one that I don't think I could have lived with. *What if...? What if, in my deep, dark despair, I had killed an innocent person while driving home drunk?* Something clicked in my brain. I might have sunk into that darker place if I hadn't met Adam.

At different points in my life, I had prayed to God for clear signs—a direction, a vision, a word, or a dream—but those things never came, or so I thought. But, what if all the negative things in my life were the signs from God to pay attention to? What if He'd been answering me all along? I would come to learn that He had been.

There is a beautiful passage in the Haruki Murakami novel, *Kafka on the Shore,* about a fifteen-year-old boy on the run. Although it doesn't directly mention God, it feels eerily like a story about the storms God puts in one's path.

Sometimes fate is like a small sandstorm that keeps changing directions. You change direction but the sandstorm chases you. You turn again, but the storm adjusts. Over and over, you play this out, like some ominous dance with death just before dawn. Why? Because this storm isn't something that blew in from far away, something that has nothing to do with you. This storm is you. Something inside of you. So, all you can do is give in to it, step right inside the storm, closing your eyes and plugging up your ears so the sand doesn't get in, and walk through it, step by step. There's no sun there, no moon, no direction, no sense of time. Just fine white sand swirling up into the sky like pulverized bones. That's the kind of sandstorm you need to imagine.

And you really will have to make it through that violent, metaphysical, symbolic storm. No matter how metaphysical or symbolic it might be, make no mistake about it: it will cut through flesh like a thousand razor blades. People will bleed there, and you will bleed too. Hot, red blood. You'll catch that blood in your hands, your own blood, and the blood of others.
And once the storm is over you won't remember how you made it through, how you managed to survive. You won't even be sure, in fact, whether the storm is really over. But one thing is certain. When you come out of the storm you won't be the same person who walked in. That's what this storm's all about.

I had weathered the storm and was ready to discover what lay ahead with my partner and co-captain. Little did I know that I was just beginning on a roller coaster ride in God's Amusement Park.

Takeaway

- When we pray, sometimes God gives us an answer by giving us yet another hoop to jump through, another hurdle. That is when we must seriously consider whether the answer is in the hurdle.

- "The grace of God" is not simply an expression. It is often precisely why good things happen and tragic mistakes are avoided.

- It's too good not to mention this again, but sometimes a setback really is the setup for your comeback.

- Even if you believe you're at your darkest place, know that you can pivot and begin your journey out of the void.

- God answers in mysterious ways.

Chapter 3

Rebirth and Reinvention

"It's never too late to be what you might have been."

George Elliot

The author Napoleon Hill, who wrote the groundbreaking book *Think and Grow Rich*, published in 1937, also wrote *Outwitting the Devil* the following year. That book, his second, was so controversial for the time that it wasn't published until seventy years later. I read it, but it wasn't until meeting Adam that I realized how it was talking directly to me.

Hill writes that there are only two bases on which we build our lives—faith and fear—and how the devil's goal is to try to keep the unhappy right where they are. That if you're nervous about changing your life for the better, that is the devil's way of telling you not to try.

All the best coaches in my life, in the next dozen or so years, told me some variation of the same thing: Your darkest days are most likely to put you on the right path. Finally, it was true for me. Finally, I was pivoting in the opposite direction of my downward spiral.

Help is Needed

Adam and I fell in love so quickly that our friends and family asked, *"Don't you think you guys need to slow it down a little bit?"*

"No," we said on separate occasions. *"When you know, you know."*

After a year together, I told him, *"It's time to make an honest woman out of me."*

We gathered with his two kids on Christmas morning a few weeks later, and he officially proposed. Four months later, we were married. Afterward, I felt more secure and protected than I ever had. To this day, he is my rock.

THE VOICE INSIDE

I think the love and contentment I finally felt created space to explore my psyche and ask questions about myself and my place in the world. I was always curious about people and behaviors and believed in God and Jesus, but I had yet to understand how both fit into my life. When Adam and I first wed, God was not at the center of our marriage or even part of our conversation, yet there had been little hints throughout my life that He had something to say to me. I went back to church and started attending regularly. Maybe I was finally in a place to listen a little more attentively.

I hadn't learned yet that I still had many destructive habits. I had not healed completely. Unfortunately, we would discover some hard truths about the church we chose, and our life together, meaning problems with his family and his ex. Which shouldn't have been surprising, given the constant demands of time and attention they placed on Adam, but I continued to bend over backward to gain their love, or at least their respect. We would later learn neither was ever going to happen regardless of what I did.

In time, Adam and I would both heal, and we would come to understand the destructive influences from both our families. After a lot of therapy and education (and still, we've never stopped, and never will) Adam also realized that he had chosen his first wife—as well as me—because he had grown up in such a toxic environment. Toxicity attracts toxicity. Cycles.

http://jocelynwreede.com/

Events occur in cycles, whether good or bad. You must have the capacity to be honest with yourself when you are in the midst of a bad cycle. Only if you can do that will you begin the difficult journey out of the dark cycles. Adam and I succeeded.

Adam and I were living in a house his parents owned, and we poured our blood, sweat, tears, and much of our own resources into fixing it up. Despite all we did, they continuously held what they considered their "immense generosity" over our heads—a red flag out of hundreds. Unfortunately, we weren't in a place to move... at least not yet.

I still suffered periodically from the panic attacks that had beset me in my teens. I was sure that my childhood trauma had also been an essential factor in my self-destructive twenties. Though I'd finally found the love of my life, I knew that the void of depression awaited me if I wasn't careful. I would need help to steer clear of that void, remain sane, and be the best partner I could be. I went to counseling—the kind that had a basis in my newly ignited faith. Although I wasn't a stranger to counseling, after years of sadness and the abuse I had endured, but until then I had never fully embraced it. Meeting Adam and gaining the support I truly needed gave me the strength to endure and persevere.

Recovery

Finding a counseling program that had Christian-centric roots was important to me. I knew that part of the answer to my recovery and strength would be found in the Bible. The story of the prophet Elijah stands out in that respect.

Elijah confronted the idolatry of the Israelites, confronted and defeated the prophets of Baal, and then faced persecution from Queen Jezebel. Afterward, he became so fearful and despairing that he sought refuge under a tree and cried out that he wanted to die. Instead, an angel gave him food and water, and God whispered to him that he would be all right. Hadn't Elijah experienced such extreme sadness and exhaustion that, today, he might be diagnosed as clinically depressed? There are many scholars and theologians who would agree with that diagnosis. However, it is purely subjective to align Elijah's experiences with clinical depression. Still, if Elijah could find himself pulled back from the brink of despair by God, couldn't I?

Around 2010, I landed at Celebrate Recovery, an excellent nationwide Christ-centered, recovery program for anyone struggling from hurts, habits, or hang-ups. There, I met people recovering from porn addiction, drug abuse, and physical and mental abuse who were totally at rock bottom. I was there to help myself, to prevent myself from falling into another bout of depression, heal, and gain greater insight into who I was as a Christian, yet I felt as though I could help those other people. Maybe God had a bigger plan for me because my own depression felt as far away as the moon. In its place, I felt a spark—more like an electrical current pass through my body—what I can only believe was a sign from God. I felt as though I was being called.

I met with my group leader in a small gathering of other women, but before long, the powers-that-be asked me to start training for leadership. Of course, I thought, *that is my calling. I'm here to help myself by helping others.*

Throughout the week, I alternated between working with my christian counselor and participating in my Celebrate Recovery group and training. Something was changing inside me. I was using everything I had gone through to try to help the women in my group. They were heartbreakingly broken. My counselor told me she couldn't believe my transformation over that first year.

"All that weight from your childhood seems to have been lifted from your shoulders. You're rising to the occasion with such grace. You are a more mature Christian right now than most people in their 60s, 70s, and 80s that I attend church with."

I was so grateful to her and the program, grateful to help the women I was assigned to, but I was also thinking, *What is happening here?* I hadn't planned on becoming a lifeline for others, but then I realized it wasn't about me anymore. I was in a place to provide service to the people around me.

At church and prayer meetings, people began to approach me to tell me that I was chosen, that I would do more, and that I was a prophet. Sometimes they would lay their hands on me while they spoke. I also had many transformational spiritual experiences. During church services, my hands would feel hot, and when I laid my hands on a friend who had been diagnosed with cancer, he went into remission. He told me he had felt the power and heat emanating from my hands.

A young woman from a church in another state came to speak at our Sunday service. When I was introduced to her, I greeted her with a handshake.

She stared at me for several seconds before saying, *"You're one of us."*
At first, I didn't know what she meant.
I wanted to joke, *"You mean an alien?"*

But in the next moment, I suddenly knew what she meant on a cellular level. I knew I was being called, and my connection to God was only strengthening.

My spiritual antenna was raised, and I was picking up signals right and left. I was not only able to identify with the women in my counseling groups, but I was also able to see how much their struggles had to do with their early lives and the abuse they suffered. I could "see" them in a way that they hadn't felt seen before. And they could hear me when I told them they didn't have to let their childhoods define them, that, in fact, they could use their struggles to propel them forward instead of pulling them back into the void.

Eyes Wide Open

In 2011, I started having a recurring dream. The dream would begin with Jesus being baptized by John the Baptist in the River Jordan, and then it would shift to me in the river being baptized by Jesus. Every night for weeks, I had the same dream, over and over. I had already been baptized as a baby, but obviously, I had no recollection of the event. I told my husband that I believed I needed to be baptized again to fully embrace my new life committed to Jesus—my rebirth, so to speak. I felt anew.

I said to Adam, *"Everything left to do on my journey in this life has to be done by the new Jocelyn. I am going to use all that has happened to me up to this point to help others. I want to move forward with a clean slate, just as I had as a brand-new baby."*

THE VOICE INSIDE

Adam listened, as he always did, and then he came up with suggestions. *"Okay,"* he said.

"How about we find a pond or a lake for your baptism?"

"No," I insisted. *"It has to be a river. My dream is telling me that I must be baptized in a river."*

As luck would have it, we went camping with our church group to the Mohican River—a beautiful forty-mile tributary in North-Central Ohio—and it was then and there that I asked my pastor to baptize me. Other people in our group decided to join me in my baptism. One of them was a little girl.

My pastor led our group down to the river. I was to go first, so I started down a deep, muddy embankment in my flip-flops. I made it a couple of feet before I fell back and slipped straight into the water.

"You're going to get baptized twice today," I heard from the assembled onlookers.

It was like a party; everyone was giddy and excited, watching expectantly from the sidelines.

The pastor came by my side, said his peace, and then lowered me down into the river, which was not as cold as I'd imagined it would be—or maybe I was not even aware of the temperature, only the gentle drift of the current. I kept my eyes wide open and saw the sun's rays flickering through the water above as though they were beaming right into me. I wanted to keep my eyes open to see my new life when I popped out of the river.

When I finally broke through the surface, the entirety of my being felt brand new. I was reborn. All the shame and pain of my past felt lifted from my heart. I was no longer afraid.

I knew that I would use everything that had happened to me to help others, so when unexplainable events started occurring after that, I just embraced them all and let Him lead me. I began to surround myself with people who, like me, were searching to grow and learn and become exactly who God designed them to be. I didn't want to waste time and energy on people who doubted my newfound identity or my faith in Jesus.

A New Identity

It's possible to be reborn, no matter what your place in life and no matter your age. Whether you're forty, fifty, or seventy, there is room for improvement and space in your heart to know God if you are willing to make the effort. Rebirth is possible for anyone who wants to become better and stronger. That is what I realized when I burst through the water and into the sun-drenched air. I also realized that I could inspire others to accept God and have the courage to make changes for the better.

THE VOICE INSIDE

Of course, I was still a sinner. But something changed. Whenever I sinned, I was struck with an immediate need to repent. I had gained awareness about who was real and who was fake. After being reborn I knew that those who mistreated me and yet weren't convicted themselves by their sin had no connection to God, regardless of what they may have claimed. This new gift of clarity continues to surprise me, as if I have developed a sort of double vision. It sits deep within me and defies explanation.

Throughout my life, I always felt like a leader, though sometimes that feeling was more a burden than an attribute, especially when my actions and beliefs defied the norm. When I decided to get baptized, that led other people to do the same. No one besides me had planned to be baptized in that river.

The sacrament of baptism is not a requirement in life. Instead, it is something personal between oneself and God. There are plenty of ways to acquire a connection to God but, for me, baptism was the most intimate way to make that connection and give myself over to Him. The fact that I did it with an audience of my congregation made me feel accountable to God and myself. It also served to mark the beginning of my reinvention.

Of course, that reinvention was a process. Let's be honest. As human beings, we can't just change the neural pathways of our brains that have formed and hard-wired over decades, but we can experience moments of crystal-clear awareness. That awareness is what can lead us to develop new neural pathways. Even if you default to the old, established ones, with awareness, you can catch yourself. Over time, your new pathways will become stronger and stronger, until, and will eventually, become your new default.

With practice and awareness, I eventually became a better person—more patient and understanding of the battles others faced. I became a better friend, a better wife, and a better mother. We can seek the courage to reinvent ourselves, to make changes, to find an awareness of self ... to be reborn. A whole new, improved life is there for the taking and the seeing.

Why Now?

You may think that you're okay where you are in your life, but there is always room for improvement because if you're not progressing, if you're not learning something new every day, and if you're not challenging yourself and your ideals, then you are probably stuck. You don't have to be an alcoholic, or an addict, or lonely, or unsuccessful to be stuck. Being stuck may manifest as a state of mind or a physical state of being.

We are all unique in our own ways. We all have our own strengths and weaknesses. We are all worthy of Him.

THE VOICE INSIDE

Once we realize that, once we believe we have the potential to change our bad habits and lifestyles, once we believe that we can up our game and achieve our goals and dreams, only then can we truly be alive. There is no reason to live a mediocre life, not at any age, not at any time.

So many people have lived through trauma and loss and difficult childhoods, me included. I'm not unique in that regard, but I realized that starting down a path of discovery and self-improvement was my assignment from a power higher than myself.

And once I started on that path, my first reaction was,

"Wow, why didn't I begin this reinvention sooner? How could I have wasted all those years in misery and self-delusion, addiction, and abuse? Why didn't I listen more when I was younger?"

The answer is that God knew I wasn't ready to listen any sooner. I wasn't prepared for His enlightenment. Everything I went through was part of the lessons I needed to learn before I was ready to be reborn and reinvent myself. As a child, I had to protect my sister. I had to witness the abuse and sometimes be the object of it. I had to rebel as a teenager and make painful mistakes. I had to stumble through my twenties, thirties, unseeing. Meanwhile, God was along for the ride, pursuing me in His own way and waiting for the moment I was ready to accept Him into my life. He knew I wouldn't be ready until I connected all the dots for myself.

When I was finally ready and willing, I found myself saying out loud,

"Okay. I give up. Let's do this."

Sometimes There is Resistance

Not everyone will be happy about your reinvention or your rebirth. And indeed, not everyone who could benefit from your guidance will be willing to accept it. Some people will resist your new, enlightened self and your attempts to help them see the light. That is only because they will feel threatened by your positive changes. After all, your positive change only underscores the fact that they are stuck.

Have the courage of your convictions and know that you are not the first to meet resistance head-on. For centuries, those who have dared to reinvent themselves have suffered the fury of people unwilling to let go of their scarcity mindsets and negativity. In other words, not everyone wants to deal with their own BS and experience rebirth.

There is a story known as Plato's Cave Allegory. It usually serves as an illustration of Plato's theory of knowledge and the nature of reality. For all intents and purposes, it is an excellent lesson on how an enlightened person, who has gone through a rebirth, might be challenged when they try to help a friend, family member, or stranger become unstuck.

The allegory begins with a group of prisoners who have been chained inside a dark cave since birth. They face a wall, unable to turn their heads. Behind them is a fire, and between the fire and the prisoners, there is a raised walkway. People outside the cave pass along the walkway, casting shadows on the wall in front of the prisoners.

Since the prisoners can only see the shadows, they believe that these shadows are the only reality and that they constitute the entirety of existence. They give names to the shadows and consider them the true forms of things.

Then, one day, a prisoner is freed and forced to turn around and face the cave entrance. Initially, the bright light outside dazzles him, and he can't comprehend the people casting the shadows. Gradually, he becomes accustomed to the light and begins to see the people. He realizes that the shadows he used to see were mere illusions of reality.

The freed prisoner then returns to the cave to share his newfound knowledge with the other prisoners. However, they can't believe there is a world beyond the shadows. They ridicule him and believe something terrible has happened to him, so they can't accept that there is anything better for them.

It is a timeless story to remember if you happen to be that freed prisoner who is fortunate enough to experience a rebirth. Some people may embrace your reinvention, and others may hate you for it. Remember that no matter how good your intentions are, you will only be able to help those who are ready or wanting your help. I found that out the hard way.

"Jesus answered, 'Truly, truly, I say to you, unless one is born of water and the Spirit, he cannot enter the kingdom of God. That which is born of the flesh is flesh, and that which is born of the Spirit is spirit. Do not marvel that I said to you, 'You must be born again.' The wind blows where it wishes, and you hear its sound, but you do not know where it comes from or where it goes. So, it is with everyone who is born of the Spirit."

John 3:5-8 ESV

As much as I felt born again, as much as I was beginning to gain an inkling that God may have had a plan for me, I felt I was in a waiting room to hear exactly what that plan was. Couldn't He give me a clear message, a sign, a map of the journey ahead? Well, I'd waited this long. I had to have patience.

Takeaway

- Love can help you create the space to explore your psyche.
- Don't be afraid to seek healthy spiritual guidance and counseling. Find a support group that jives with your belief system.
- Commit to your reinvention once you find your way. Baptism is a beautiful way to set you on your path, but it is not the only way.
- Understand that reinvention is a process. It takes time to break down the neural pathways that took years to create. Be patient. Stick to it.
- At any point in your life, you can better yourself. There is no expiration date on self-knowledge.
- Not everyone will be pleased with the new, improved you. Be strong and proceed.

Chapter 4

I Am Called

"I need for you to understand that you are not defined by the awful things that happened to you. That traumatic childhood, that abusive boyfriend, that cheating spouse, that friend who betrayed you ... those experiences are not all of you. Certainly, a part of you, but not all of you. They are not who you are."

One of my Mentors-
Jennifer Allwood

I always felt a strong affinity for Biblical stories concerning children because, looking back, there were moments in my own childhood when I could see that God was guiding me. Almost everyone knows the Bible story of how

THE VOICE INSIDE

God called upon Moses to free the Israelites, but a lesser-known story about being called by God concerns a young boy named Samuel.

Samuel served in the tabernacle under the high priest, Eli, during a time when few people could lay claim to hearing the voice of God.

While Samuel was sleeping in the tabernacle one night, he heard a voice call, "Samuel!" Believing that Eli must have called for him, he ran to him to see what he wanted. Eli told Samuel that he hadn't called him and told him to go back to sleep.

Throughout the night, Samuel heard the same voice call his name three more times. Each time, he thought it was Eli's voice. Finally, Eli realized it was God calling Samuel. God advised Samuel to answer. *"Speak, Lord, for your servant is listening."*

When Samuel heard the voice again, he answered as Eli told him to. God then revealed His message: He would bring judgment upon the house of Eli because Eli's sons had been wicked.

From that moment on, Samuel became a prophet, relaying the voice of God. Samuel heard God in the quiet of the night and was finally able to understand and respond.

The story of Samuel was a lesson to me that God might very well, at some point, have a message for me if I were willing to listen, even in the most unlikely moments. I would have to keep my antennae up and my mind ready to accept.

A Search for Meaning

One afternoon, I was sitting in my counselor's waiting room, listening to a local station on the radio. The announcer started talking about a prayer vigil in town for a teenager who had died in a car accident. I didn't know the teenager or his family, but I told Adam that I felt a pull to attend. At the time, I had been reading the book, *The Boy Who Came Back from Heaven*, by Kevin Malarkey, an account about his son's experience in Heaven after a traffic accident. Once I decided to attend the prayer vigil, I found out that the book's author was to be there—a strange coincidence—so I decided to bring my copy, as well.

At the vigil, I ran into a distant cousin. I was as surprised to see him as he was to see me. Before I could ask whether he knew the deceased, he asked me why I was there.

The first thing out of my mouth was, *"God sent me here."*

My answer felt involuntary, but I told the same to anyone who asked. In turn, everyone responded by looking at me like I had three heads, but I didn't care. That's the thing with feeling called; I was there because I needed to be there, and I had no fear of what anyone thought of my reasoning.

After the service, I approached the author and asked him to sign my book.

Inside the cover he wrote:

"And call upon me in the day of trouble; I will deliver you, and you shall glorify me."

Psalm 50:15 ESV

It was as if he were describing my life in a nutshell, right there. *Another sign?* I wondered.

When I got home, it was nearly eleven p.m., and Adam was ready to go to bed, but I wanted to finish *The Boy Who Came Back from Heaven.* I told Adam to go ahead, that I didn't have many pages left. He went to sleep, and I sat in the living room, reading a section of the book where the boy describes praying against demons. Right there and then, I decided to try doing the same. I figured, no time like the present. I prayed hard, asking God to protect my family and my home against anything demonic that might try to enter. Then I finished the book and went to bed.

I tried to sleep, but my mind was racing. As much as I wanted to discuss all the thoughts swirling through my head, I didn't want to wake Adam. He sleeps with a CPAP (Continual Positive Airway Pressure machine)—a device that keeps your airways open while you sleep so you can receive the oxygen you need to reduce your health risks and improve sleep quality—and looked too peaceful to disturb. The CPAP was humming along, making its usual blowing noises. Except for that and Adam's breathing, the house was quiet.

Suddenly, out of the ether, it seemed, I heard a swishing noise followed by what sounded like the slamming of doors. I then heard my name and a strong male voice. I looked over at Adam, but he was still sound asleep, I could no longer hear his machine or anything in the house. Then I heard it again but clearly this time.

The voice said, *"I have inscribed a place for you in the church,"* and then repeated itself.
"What do you mean?" I asked aloud to no one in particular. *"Inscribed? My writing?"*
A resounding, *"Yes,"* filled the room.

I felt as if cold water had been thrown on me. It had to be Him. God was in that room with me and Adam.

I tried to remain calm, but I felt alarmed and confused. *"What? Who? Me?"* I asked. *"You mean me?"*

THE VOICE INSIDE

Anyone who thinks God doesn't have a sense of humor is sadly mistaken. I could hear Him chuckling, and then He answered, *"Yes, you."*

All I could say was, *"I don't want this. I don't want this!"*

Before I could grasp the immensity of the conversation, my husband started choking under the grip of his CPAP mask. He awoke, ripped off the mask, and made a beeline for the bathroom as I chased after him. He continued to gasp for air, but now so violently that he fell to the ground and hit his head on the way down. I grabbed my phone as Adam struggled to breathe. If I dialed 911 and spent precious minutes on the phone, would an ambulance even get here in time to save my husband? I put down the phone and started praying.

"Oh, God," I said. *"Please, not now. Not now. Don't do this, please."*

I prayed as hard as I could for Adam to resume normal breathing. I felt I was fighting the demons threatening to take my husband away from me. They were trying to choke him to death to retaliate for the cleansing I'd done. No doubt for the conversation with God I just had.

Within seconds, Adam started breathing on his own as though the moments before were in the distant past. We looked at each other as if to say, "What the hell just happened?" Adam shrugged. Never one to sweat the small stuff, or to overthink a situation, he said that he was going back to bed. And he did. He slept like a baby until the morning.

I spent the rest of the night on the bathroom floor, googling "scribed," "scribe and Bible," and "What does it mean to scribe in Biblical terms?"

What was God trying to tell me to do?

God is Chasing Me

When God had first spoken to me, my response had seemed anything but enthusiastic. *Why me?* Those were the first words out of my mouth. But it wasn't the intimacy with Him I didn't want. I didn't want the responsibility of what it would mean to be on the receiving end of God's word.

By morning, however, my feelings had changed. I realized the awesome truth that God had audibly spoke to me. Had it been a mere coincidence that this happened just when I needed Him? Did I not trust my senses because I simply felt unworthy, still at this point in my life? I looked at the quote from Exodus, Chapter 4, that I had recently taped to my refrigerator. "God does not call the qualified. He qualifies those he calls." Of course. My mind started reeling.

THE VOICE INSIDE

That Sunday at church, I told my pastor and his wife everything that had happened. Between them, they had had several experiences with angels, visions, and demons. My pastor said they were at a prayer meeting in another state on the night God spoke to me.

"What time were you reading that book and praying against those demons?" he asked.

When I told him, he laughed. I must have looked confused because he explained, *"At the exact moment you were praying against those demons, the spiritual elders and I were having a conversation about you."*

I was floored. *"Why? What do you mean?"*

"Well," he said, *"I was telling them about you, and they said, 'She's got to be one of them, one of the chosen. And she's going to get more messages.'"*

That was all I needed to hear. I had definitely not imagined hearing God. From then on, I started to quiet my mind and pay more attention to the signs in my life. It was as though I had permission to feel the connection that was there all along—a connection to a realm we can't see. My belief in Him was completely solidified. I always knew I was destined to share God's word with the world. Now I understood that what I had heard was real.

Soon after the night, God told me to scribe. I happened to be standing at my kitchen sink, washing dishes. I was staring out the window, daydreaming, when I felt a hand on my back—every single finger, as if the hand was propping me up and keeping me from falling. Thinking it was my husband, I whipped around, but no one was there. I sucked in my breath slowly, surely.

This time, I understood. God was confirming my understanding.

Sharing His Word

It wasn't more than a couple of weeks later when I was at church with my husband and young son. It was a Sunday, much like every other Sunday. We were all in our pews, listening to the pastor and singing the hymns. As the service began, our pastor asked if anyone had any prayer requests, as was a standard question every Sunday.

Our congregation was small—maybe forty people at any given time—and I generally knew everyone there. A woman I'd never spoken to more than to say, "Good morning," stood up to share.

She seemed upset, her voice shaking as she began to talk.

THE VOICE INSIDE

"I was sent to the hospital this week because I have not been feeling good. I had a terrible headache, so my husband drove me to the hospital, and they told me I have a brain tumor." She started to well up but continued speaking. *"I'm going to ... Cleveland Clinic this week for another opinion."*

It was apparent she couldn't say another word, lest she'd break down.

When it was the pastor's turn to speak, he opened his mouth, I heard the same whooshing sound of a strong wind and then doors slamming shut like I'd heard in my bedroom that night. I shook my head and pressed my ears. When I looked up at the pastor, I could see his lips moving, but I couldn't hear a word he was saying. I couldn't hear anything, not the pastor, not the rustling of people in their seats or the parents shushing their fidgeting kids. I grabbed my head, thinking I'd gone suddenly deaf.

My husband saw how panicked I was and asked, *"What's wrong? Jocelyn, what's wrong?"*

But I couldn't hear his voice, either. I was reading his lips, as though I was in a silent movie.

In the next moment, I somehow knew that I was okay and that I needed to pay attention, so I put my hand up for him to calm down.

Just then, I heard a powerful male voice, like the one I'd listened to that night in my room. *"Go tell her that no matter what, everything is going to be okay,"* the voice said several times.

Later, my husband would tell me that I just about knocked him clean off the pew as I pushed past him to make my way to the woman and her husband. I knew she was the one I needed to give my message to. It had to be her.

To her husband's and the entire congregation's surprise, I wrapped my arms around the woman and whispered in her ear, *"I'm supposed to tell you that no matter what, everything is going to be okay."*

The woman, whose name was Linda, started sobbing as she hugged me back. Her husband looked as though he'd seen a ghost.

He thanked me and said, *"Please, tell us if you hear anything more. Please, let us know."*

If I hear anything more. They believed I was offering the word of God. After the service, I explained to my bewildered pastor what I'd heard. He smiled and reminded me that it was just as the elders had determined; I was a prophet.

Everything that was happening to me was all part of God's plan for me.

When the next Sunday rolled around, the pastor greeted me at the door and said, *"Have you talked to Linda? Have you heard?"*

"What? No, I don't know what you're talking about," I said.

He didn't want to tell me any news ahead of time, so he told me to wait until Linda addressed the congregation.

The service began with Linda. She stood up and told us that she'd been to the Cleveland Clinic that week and that they ran further tests. She didn't have a brain tumor, but she did have an early-stage Parkinson's. They'd also told her that the best therapy was dance—ironically, she was a dance instructor. She was more hopeful than she had been since the onset of her headaches, which now seemed manageable.

That was it. After that incident, I realized that I could accomplish whatever I wanted in my life. God had given me the green light. I didn't have to remain stuck under any old labels I'd put on myself or that anyone else had either. I could choose the relationships I wanted to nurture, the ones I wanted to keep, and discard those that were weighing me down. I was enough as I was. I was called, not because I was qualified, but because God had wanted to qualify me.

Renewed Relationships

Not everyone in my life was able to comprehend what was happening to me or why I had been chosen, and it certainly wasn't my place to convince them. I realized that I had to put my ego aside to listen and find guidance to ask better questions and be open to answers that I might not have expected. Certain relationships had to be cast aside in doing so, but other relationships needed to be retained and nurtured.

Although it had taken me a lifetime, I was finally able to listen with an open heart and mind. That accomplishment allowed me to see how amazing people are, whose faith had been unwavering for their entire lives. It just took me some time to appreciate them and circle back.

My aunt had been a missionary in music ministry for over forty years. At age 12, she had a rapidly growing tumor on her vocal cords, the tissue was unrecognizable by the dr's at two different hospitals. She eventually had surgery to remove the tumor. The doctor had told her, "I hope you're not a singer because you won't be able to sing" He thought there was a possibility she wouldn't even be able to talk again without the help of a device. When she went back for her checkup a couple weeks later, there was no remnant of any surgery on her vocal chords, no scar tissue, nothing. The dr. was baffled. It looked as though her vocal cords had been miraculously healed. And that's exactly what my aunt knew had happened. God had healed her vocal cords.

She went on to accomplish so much in her life and lead worship in song to the nations, something the doctors had told her she would never be able to do.

Her mother, my grandma, had her own healing experience. Grandma had had a severe case of colitis in her forties. Because there was no cure then, her doctors had scheduled surgery to give her a colostomy.

The night before the surgery, God woke her from a dead sleep and said, *"Get down beside your bed and kneel. Ask me to heal you, and I will."* He repeated the message even asking her to please kneel beside the bed and ask this of him.

And so, she did what He said, and then she went back to sleep.

When she arrived for her surgery, she was pain-free for the first time in a long while. On further examination, her doctor determined that her colitis was gone. It was as though she'd never even had it.

The grace of God had healed both women. All I could think was, *Man, is this in my family? Am I part of a chosen lineage?*

It stood to reason that as similar incidents played out in my life, I went to my aunt and grandmother for guidance—my aunt, especially. She became one of my closest spiritual mentors because she understood everything I was going through. She knew that my life's "strange occurrences" were due to things beyond this physical realm.

"It takes one strong woman of faith to know another," she told me.

So cool, I thought. So cool and so believably miraculous.

What We Cannot See

For most of my life, I instinctively knew there was something more than what was presented to me in this physical world. I was going to preface that by saying, "Except for when I was in my darkest hours," but I think that, in those dark hours, God was beside me, as well, forcing me out of bed, hung over and despairing, to hear His words eventually. After hearing and accepting those words, I knew He meant for me to share them with the world. I knew He wanted me to serve others—friends, family, strangers. How could I deny the Creator of The Universe? Obviously, I had tried that after my divorce, but He chased me down and wore me out. I can only thank Him for not giving up on me and for continuing to call until I was ready to listen.

THE VOICE INSIDE

I'm often asked how or why God called me, or what it takes to receive the same calling. I don't have an answer to those questions, but I do know that to hear a calling, one must be able to listen, and I don't mean just with one's ears. I mean the kind of listening that takes place deep inside. The listening that happens when you're not so focused on the minutiae of daily life and the petty dramas that seem to play out daily around you.

Once you can look deep within and give yourself over to faith and trust in God, then it is possible to hear what He wants you to hear. That doesn't mean you will get everything you ask for, at least not all at once. You may find your answers in bits and pieces and in ways you were not expecting. What's important is that you consider what you may not be able to see with your eyes, which is difficult because we usually only see what we know. It's the unknown that we need to know, the unknown that we need to recognize.

Those coincidences and moments of great insight in your life? Recognize them as breadcrumbs leading you out of the forest and to the light. Don't dismiss what can't be explained or make less of the power in a moment of clarity. *Oh, it's just a coincidence. Oh, I didn't really hear that voice. Oh, that's not possible.*

If you believe in a power greater than yourself, you can run through fire. You can move mountains or, at least, push yourself to do more extraordinary things than you ever thought possible. It's like having a Superman cape. That's how I look at it. God has my back, and nothing here can stop me from doing anything I set my mind to.

Why wouldn't you choose to up your game, relationships, and life? Why wouldn't you choose to give up your anger and blame and find happiness? The only reason you wouldn't choose those things is if you're attached to your misery and pain or don't feel worthy of something better. Well, you are worthy. You just need someone to tell you that, so consider me the messenger.

One of my favorite stories to remember is the following, "Footprints in the Sand," by Mary Stevenson:

One night I dreamed a dream.
As I was walking along the beach with my Lord.
Across the dark sky flashed scenes from my life.
For each scene, I noticed two sets of footprints in the sand,
One belonging to me and one to my Lord.
After the last scene of my life flashed before me,
I looked back at the footprints in the sand.
I noticed that at many times along the path of my life,
especially at the very lowest and saddest times,
there was only one set of footprints.
This really troubled me, so I asked the Lord about it.

THE VOICE INSIDE

"Lord, you said once I decided to follow you,
You'd walk with me all the way.
But I noticed that during the saddest and most troublesome
times of my life,
there was only one set of footprints.
I don't understand why, when I needed You the most, You
would leave me."
The LORD replied:
"My precious child, I love you and will never leave you
Never, ever, during your trials and suffering.
When you saw only one set of footprints,
It was then that I carried you."

God had followed me. He had carried me, and He had
never left my side. I owed it to Him to spread His word and
help others break their own cycles of abuse. I would try, but it
wouldn't be easy. Nothing worthwhile ever is.

<u>Takeaway</u>

- Never be afraid to ask for help. Seek out the help you
  need, whether it is through mental health services or
  spiritual counseling. Take that first step. Strength is
  getting help.
- There are no coincidences. Learn not to dismiss those
  things you label as such. Look for the signs in your life

that He is with you. God may be guiding you without your knowledge.

- Don't be afraid to speak if and when the Spirit moves you, especially if it means helping your fellow woman or man. Have the courage of your convictions.

- Re-evaluate. After you've sought help and feel on the path to healing, don't be afraid to revisit relationships you may have neglected or dismissed. Be willing to apologize, repair, and regain love.

- Some things in life can't be explained, but that doesn't mean you should ignore them. Keep your eyes, ears, and heart open. Only then will you not miss the signs.

Chapter 5

Life's Cycles

"And this is the judgment: the light has come into the world, and people loved the darkness rather than the light because their works were evil. For everyone who does wicked things hates the light and does not come to the light, lest his works should be exposed. But whoever does what is true comes to the light, so that it may be clearly seen that his works have been carried out in God."

John 3:19-21 ESV

Life is full of cycles. They represent the natural rhythms and patterns that shape us. There are cycles in nature, relationships, personal growth, and society. Obviously, we humans don't have much of a say in changing the cycles of birth and death. We can't alter the seasons or the ebb and flow of rivers, but we can adjust the emotional and psychological cycles we find ourselves in. We can make a choice—through personal growth, self-awareness, and resilience—to change the negative cycles in our lives. We can break cycles of fear and abuse and foster connections with people who want to help us do the same. Alternatively, we can sever ties with those who might want to pull us into their own negative cycles.

We all have it in us to evolve and transform ourselves. We all have the power deep within to choose the positive over the negative, good over evil, and love over fear. It just takes time, commitment, and a good dose of courage, especially when breaking a cycle of abuse.

You don't have to fall into the trap of treating your partner as your parents treated theirs or treating your child as you were treated. You don't have to be the abuser or the abused just because those were the roles modeled to you. If you haven't already done so, it's time to break those generational curses that have been handed down to you. Don't inherit what you don't want.

I'm not saying that's an easy thing to do. It's difficult to break through your hard-wired default behavior, which is why most people don't even try. It means having to think twice and three times in order to make better life and better relationship decisions. It means fighting specific autopilot responses you've had since childhood. It may mean seeking spiritual counsel, support, and therapy to make the transition, but believe me; it is worth it.

Everyone wants what is easy in life, but as you've probably heard before, the hardest things to accomplish are the most rewarding.

The Cycle of Dysfunction

Adam may have been my knight in shining armor but finding him did not initiate a happily ever after. Like me, he had a difficult time after his divorce. It had not ended well, despite his best intentions and efforts to maintain a healthy, working relationship with his ex.

Abruptly, I found myself thrust into the role of the evil stepmother, though not by my choice or deeds. Adam did everything he could to welcome me into his family, but his children were not keen on doing the same, and neither were his parents.

In our brief courtship, I had learned how much Adam's kids meant to him. They were his world, which meant I wanted them to be an essential part of mine.

By the time Adam and I were married, his two kids were shuttling back and forth, every other week, from their mother's house to ours. It quickly became apparent that his ex-wife was not only poisoning them against me but also trying to drive a wedge into Adam's relationship with them. Parental alienation.

Adam's parents were not only not helping matters; they were exacerbating the problem. They, too, were doing their best to make me the bad guy in the equation.

Adam's kids would lash out in anger at the two of us, parroting insults and accusations they'd quite obviously picked up from their mother and grandparents. I knew that pain was the true source of their anger, so as hurtful as their tirades were, I tried my best not to take them personally. What I thought truly unconscionable was that adults would want to perpetuate unhappiness in their children and grandchildren. Why would anyone want to continue that kind of cycle of dysfunction? We eventually came to know the answer.

It took many years, before Adam's daughter finally came to the light. It took a lot of patience on my and Adam's end and a certain amount of faith on her part. She was about 18 years old when the shift began. She finally saw that Adam and I weren't the enemy, and that her mother and grandparents were the real instigators of unhappiness in their lives.

Even though it is unnecessary, she often apologizes for her behavior and the behavior of others. Her sincerity brings us to tears, but she feels the need to express the guilt and shame she feels for not seeing the truth. After many years of anguish and prayer, we finally have a close personal relationship that touches my heart.

Though it is difficult for us all, she has decided to move her family to Vermont, so she can distance herself and her children from the toxicity here and break the cycles of abuse. She wants her children to be free of the pain she suffered as a child into her adulthood and even today. Her wish is that we will join them, so we can all continue together the work of healing and growing that we all began together. I do not have a crystal ball, but it is definitely within the realm of possibility. Like her dad, she has the strength and drive to understand how toxic relationships of the past can tarnish her future.

I was personally inspired when she ended the cycle of anger and distrust she had been handed, even if it took as long as it did. She took her journey at her own pace, and we are proud of her for facing it.

We also hope and pray that Adam's son will truthfully understand what has had happened throughout those years and still, and how all those events shaped his beliefs. Our belief systems are created for us as children, its up to us to clean that filter and properly heal in order to be able to navigate our own perceptions correctly.

When children are damaged, the effects can be lifelong and crippling. Even so, all is not necessarily lost. A grown child who has remained stuck can still begin a journey to know the truth, to heal, and to throw off the chains of fear and shame.

True, the path to the truth is not easy. Being brutally honest with yourself, looking unflinchingly at your life, and building a new life of truth and understanding is demanding. But the ultimate reward is happiness and peace and worth the fight. I know because I've done it.

Halting a Cycle

I made one of the most significant transformations of my life fourteen years ago when I became a mother. Thankfully, Adam was excited at the idea of having a child with me, but the decision was one I agonized over because I was afraid. I was worried that I would become the parent my father and stepfather had been. I was scared to be the abandoner or the abuser. What if I perpetuated the same cycle that I'd been a part of as a child?

Years after my mother divorced my stepfather, his son and daughter from a previous marriage re-entered my life. His daughter and I contacted each other, and I found out from her that her younger brother had been the target of her father's beatings when he was drunk. As the older and stronger sibling, she managed to avoid much of the physical abuse. Not surprisingly, it also turned out that my stepfather was a victim of abuse from his father—a cycle three times.

I needn't have worried about my decision to have a child, because I fell madly in love with my son at first sight and instantly assumed the role of protector—the role I believe God had always intended for me.

What did happen was that I experienced a renewed anger toward my biological father. I couldn't possibly imagine how he, or anyone else for that matter, could deny their own child. I couldn't imagine walking away from my beautiful boy, no matter how ill-equipped I felt.

Eventually, I understood my anger wouldn't serve me or my family. I don't know if I actually forgave my biological father for walking out on his family, but I did reach the point where I no longer felt anger or bitterness toward him—rather, I only felt sorry for him. He hadn't the courage or the strength to face up to his own demons and be the father I needed him to be. He wasn't fortunate enough to have the family he could have had, and I found myself pitying him. Another cycle was broken.

There is No Fighting Narcissism

"After the fog lifts and you awaken to the truth about abuse, the narcissists and flying monkeys will minimize the facts about what took place. They will discredit you. They will undermine your own perception. They will accuse you of

*being insane. Even if you took the time to explain yourself,
they will cast all blame onto you."*

Dana Arcuri

As part of my education after hitting rock bottom, I immersed myself in the study of psychology. I needed to understand why people were who they were and did what they did, and the causes and treatments for deep-seated pathological/psychological and emotional issues. The issue of narcissism held a particular fascination for me. My Christian counselor had first mentioned it in that certain members of Adam's family were displaying signs of it. The more I studied, and eventually with experts in the field, the more I saw that my in-laws exhibited the worst traits of not only narcissism, but also other mental illnesses and disorders. Which we later would learn ran in both of their families. Its common to have more than one.

The manifestations of their dysfunction became apparent in how they dealt with Adam's kids—their grandchildren. They would often use them to manipulate their son, Adam. Nothing they did or said was ever at face value, always part of a much bigger picture and covert agenda. So many strange occurences. Adam's father had once told our neighbor in all sincerity that he was the "master" of this family, and that his son better abide by his word. The neighbor was blown away, but we weren't surprised at all.

Adam's parents were manipulative and would often resort to shaming as a tactic of many in order to harness control. They seemed to take pleasure in triangulating by getting their children and grandchildren to take their side. Though it was easy after the years of grooming that had already taken place. They often used this tactic and did it with Adam's children especially. We also saw them try to do it with our son.

When our son was only five years old, his grandmother sat him down at their kitchen table and had him write their cell phone number over and over again so that he could memorize it. Not only did he not have a cell phone of his own at 5 years of age, he didn't yet know Adam's or my number, either.

The purpose of the exercise we would learn, was to train our son to call them instead of calling us. This type of grooming behavior can be hard to detect. It's a very long and subtle process to gain trust, but it's no different than cult like behavior, the very same tactics are used in both situations. People who are practicing these techniques know how to make it hard for others to see or easy to explain away. They were trying to triangulate our little family as they had done with my stepchildren. Cycles. Their drive was to be the most important people in our son's life because this is what allows them to exert control. To feed that need for adoration and attention. A quick internet search for expert advice from people like Dr. Phil shows that people with these personality problems are habitual liars and rarely if ever change. Once you understand the truth, there is no room to tolerate such abuse. You'll never unsee it again.

As angry as I was at that time, I knew their behaviors had to do with some dysfunction and/or trauma—trauma, insecurity, low self-esteem, and genetics are all factors in the development of a narcissistic personality disorder. My father-in-law, a belligerent and insensitive man, had experienced a devastating loss when his own father had been accidentally shot. He and his brother had been out hunting with their father when his brother had mistaken his father for a deer. Their father was killed instantly. While I felt sorry for that 6-year-old little boy who had tragically witnessed his father die, I did not feel sorry for the 70 some-year-old man he had become because he never had the will or strength to seek help. Instead, he sought to lord over everyone in his life. The disconnect in the way we witnessed him treat animals alone was disturbing enough to run like hell.

As for Adam's mother, I would have to write several books to fully illustrate all the evil things she's done. Much of her behavior was covertly passive and hidden but still intended to harm. She did what she could to appear as the innocent, doting mother and grandma. She used introverted tactics and behaviors. By contrast, her husband was very extroverted and open with hostility. Known as a Cluster B personality, it can take on many forms.

Most likely, from what we learned, she developed her capacity for psychological abuse from over-nurturing, for example, when a parent holds a child up on a pedestal. This kind of passive, invisible abuse affects the same underdeveloped areas of the brain as those in children who experience trauma. Her passive aggression doesn't go as unnoticed as she thinks it does though. This is often the outcome when a person finds the strength to break free from psychological abuse, otherwise known as the hidden abuse, but isn't all abuse hidden? Or so the perpetrators believe. Once the weakness of the tyrant is exposed, your no longer caught in a trap of fear. Sadly, the weak and unhealed often stay stuck and remain patsies in that game. Perhaps the real tragedy is that those unable to escape often share the same traits and continue the cycles of abuse from the grooming and the fact it's their "normal".

I'll give you one example of hundreds or thousands of how this kind of behavior made us want to run like hell. Adam's mother once gave us some things she found while she was doing some cleaning. She was a hoarder, which is a red flag for mental health issues. I knew there had to be some underlying motive behind the "things" she was willingly letting go of, because this type of "giving" with strings attached is common behavior for people with these personality defects.

One of the things she was giving away was Adam's baby book. I was enjoying thumbing through it, seeing pictures of his bright, fire-engine-red lock of hair, pictures of him as an infant, etc. As I began reading what his mother had written, something felt very "off." One passage in the book asked, "What was your first thought when you saw your newborn baby boy for the first time?" The written reply, her own handwritten words, was, "Oh My God! How ugly!" Even if that statement had been true, no mother in her right mind would ever say such a thing about her brand-new baby, let alone write it in a baby book.

Another red flag story of MANY occurred when I was at my sister's softball game. My mom was talking to a dear family friend, an older woman who was respected in the community as a spiritual mentor. This family friend had seemed upset, so my mom asked her what was wrong. The family friend went on to say that my mother-in-law had told her that Adam and I were getting a divorce. My mom looked puzzled and told her that definitely wasn't true. They went on to talk and realized that because my husband and I were involved in a class at church to strengthen marriages, my mother-in-law told the family friend we were getting divorced.

In fact, in conversations with us, she routinely called our class our "Divorce Class." We tried several times to explain to her that it was a class for any couple married or not to learn how to connect better and deepen their marriages through Christ. But being required to repeatedly explain is another red flag. Needless to say, we were furious. Our friend was in tears because she loves us so much, as we do her. She actually had been a wise mentor for us throughout the years of abuse and manipulation from my in-laws because she knew them well and had known and seen things herself that gave her the perspective and insight to question the health of the relationships, we were trapped in.

As I will discuss later in this book, she told us that my mother-in-law had told her at church years before that something awful had happened to her girls, but she didn't elaborate. The day she told this secret to my mom, my sister, and I in her kitchen, I got so sick it felt like someone had punched me in the gut, my knees became weak, and I nearly fell to the floor. They said the color just left my face and I was white. Because I knew exactly what that "something" was.

These bizarre and outlandish incidents piled up over the years. Similar events became common occurrences in our lives--the erratic words, the actions of endearment with no emotion or feeling behind them, the list is endless. In time, we came to learn that these types of personalities have a genuine disconnect resulting from an underdevelopment in the brain to actual emotion.

People with this dysfunction don't have the capacity to actually put themselves in another's place—in other words, they lack empathy. Any type of endearing act they portray to anyone isn't motivated by a genuine feeling. Instead, they are like actors playing a part. They learn at a very young age how to mimic the behavior of others. Even tears are fake, with no emotional connection in the brain. Understanding that psychological break explained so much for us. The pieces of the puzzle were finally beginning to come together. The years of questions about why this or why that, about why there were so many strange occurrences were beginning to paint a very unsettling story.

It would prove to be hellishly difficult to get this problem out of our lives, thanks to the giant web of lies that had already been created by these cycles of abuse. What makes breaking the cycle so difficult is that where you find one person with this personality type, you will find many more not only in the family, but among those with whom they routinely associate. Such people must keep certain types of individuals near them to be able to keep feeding their need for control— people who are weaker and who can be easily fooled and groomed. This is a profile of psychological abuse, and one wonders whether the term, "Birds of a feather flock together," was a reference to those psychological cycles of abuse.

After much struggle and effort, we finally put some distance between us and my in-laws. No doubt, God had paved the way in answer to our prayers. Throughout the long process of moving and long after, my in-laws used many underhanded tactics to punish us for rising above the trap of the abuse. They enlisted in their efforts everyone they could find, including Adam's own children. For example, they threatened to take us to court to gain visitation rights with our son. We went to the courthouse to speak with a judge to make sure nothing like that could happen. The judge assured us that because my husband and I were both living and had a happy and healthy marriage, there was no way for my in-laws to intrude. Regardless, we filled out the paperwork for a restraining order. Unfortunately, Adam decided not to proceed with the order because the judge told us there would be a court appearance with Adam's parents, which he didn't want.

Before finally getting out from under their grasp Adam had repeatedly tried to set healthy boundaries. But my in-laws only stomped on and disregarded them, over and over and over. Ultimately, my in-laws had to be removed from our lives for us to have a peaceful and healthy existence. Today, no one gets access to the inner sanctum unless they align with our core values and convictions. PERIOD. The inner sanctum is a healthy place and is very small for a reason.

Most people will never do the work they need to do to heal. Instead, they only tell themselves they do, but they never really go the distance, and develop the capacity to be honest with themselves, which is the only way to effect any real change. Most people are unwilling to humble themselves because they are weak and groomed. Let' face it—it's easier to conform to the limits society sets than to go on a self-discovery journey to find your true self and to become truly intimate with God.

Although we cannot change what people do, we can protect ourselves and our families. Don't waste your life believing the picture that someone else painted you into. IF you do not man up and do the hard work that is necessary for success, you will regret it someday. Don't lose the opportunity to become the person you were truly created to be. You risk a life of meaninglessness, plagued by the unhealthy cycles that you will pass down to your own children. If you don't believe me, God will show you, whether or not you are willing.

Never-ending Trauma

There was so much drama swirling around me in those early years of marriage. As if the stress of my husband's bitter ex-wife, (who came from dysfunction herself; i.e.cycles), the resentment his kids felt as a result, and my in-laws' attempts to manipulate, groom, and triangulate them weren't enough, Adam's sister seemed to be losing a grasp on reality. Given her parents, it wasn't surprising, but the timing was.

Her behavior had suddenly become even more erratic than normal. She began dressing in bright, loud colors decidedly unlike her usual more muted tastes. Out in public and unprovoked, she would yell at people and call them obscene names. Or even hit strangers! It may seem unbelievable, but I knew something was wrong before anyone else. I knew the signs of mental illness, especially in dysfunctional families.

Finally, everyone recognized that something was dangerously wrong. We took her to a psychologist who diagnosed her with bipolar disorder. I wasn't surprised by the diagnosis, but I was surprised by one of the suggested treatments. The psychologist insisted that she go for electroconvulsive therapy (ECT)—better known as shock treatments—where the brain is subjected to an electrically-induced seizure. I told my mother-in-law that nothing good could come from that type of treatment but, of course, she ignored me. She insisted on following the doctor's recommendations exactly as ordered. Even though we were already unhappy with this particular dr's treatment protocols.

We would learn that her insistence was a bigger piece of a covert plan. They secretly saw a benefit in keeping her ill, so they could continue the charade necessary to maintain control. She was an easy target. Instead of a treatment program of in-depth therapy, she wanted a "fix" for her daughter that would silence her, as though that would solve a lifetime of trauma. One of their more extreme plans that we heard repeatedly was to lock her up in a state mental hospital, a plan motivated by a 40-year-long effort to hide dark family secrets. She insisted on ECT treatment for her daughter because she hoped it would keep memories buried. Instead, all that resulted was the opening of a Pandora's Box of repressed memories. The brain automatically protects us by shoving traumatic events to the backs of our brains. Sadly, when traumatic events are not allowed to be processed, we become sick and unhealthy.

Adam's sister came out of the ECT treatment literally swinging, and with old, unlocked memories. She now remembered that at ages eight and ten, she and her sister had been raped by three members of a local high school football team. She described the account in great detail, right down to the sundresses they were wearing, and the identical football jerseys the abusers were wearing. The football players were driving a pale green Mustang Fastback to the summer BBQ in the summer of 1973, just outside Waynesfield, Ohio. She described the blood that was running down both of their legs. She told us about her recollection first. It was a grueling, gory, heart-wrenching, and violent account. They ran back home after the attack, cleaned up the best they could, and hid in a closet. Their parents found them there, and that was the end of it. But for the children, it was only the beginning. They would go on to develop behavioral problems and unhealthy relationships of their own, not even knowing that the repressed memories of a violent trauma were to blame.

Adam, his sister's husband confronted their parents together. Both immediately reacted defensively by calling their daughter an effing liar. These verbal attacks and accusations would continue for years. They didn't want to hear another word, which indicated that they knew something they weren't telling us. They lied about things our brother-in-law had heard them say about us while in the company of other family members on several occasions. Blatantly telling him no they didn't. Our brother-in-law was in total disbelief. He told them he had heard them say the very words he had reported with his own ears, but they denied everything. Of course, gaslighting is a common tactic used by emotional predators. In short, our meeting that day changed everything forever because we knew then for certain that we weren't dealing with healthy people—we were dealing with monsters.

We needed to take action because Adam's parents were mute to his sister's cries for help. Therefore, we went to the county sheriff's office where the crime occurred, to report the rapes. The burden was too heavy, and reporting the crime would at least relieve us of carrying the load any further. It was too heavy a burden to bear.

The detective we spoke with was floored but sympathetic, although it would be difficult, he said, to find justice in two forty-five-year-old rape cases. One of Adam's sisters would have to come forward, but neither was willing. In fact, only one of them remembered the attack. Everyone was intimidated by what other people might say. They were also too far under the spell of their parents and grandparents to act on their own behalf. Everyone so bonded to trauma and dysfunction that even though it continued to damage them, they were unwilling to rise up. Their suffering continues to this day and stands as a testament to sad, dysfunctional enmeshment at its finest.

We are genuinely blessed that with the opportunity to write this book, those innocent little girls who were given no voice now have been given a voice after 50 years of forced silence. We often wonder how many more victims those three boys/men went on to traumatize, or whether they may still be actively abusing others. We also wonder how many times we may have shaken their hands, or perhaps broken bread with them as a small community.

Not knowing who you truly are is a tragic fate. Even worse, so many people settle for mediocrity and lies because of a society that teaches us that standing in your truth is a bad thing or that going against the grain is wrong. This drive to encourage mindless conformity must change. Children like those poor little girls who were forced to suffer silently for so long are a dime a dozen anymore, and that is truly a disgrace. All the people who hide, enable, protect, and stay silent about abuse are the scum of the earth, and put simply, mere cowards.

We recently saw the movie *Sound of Freedom* depicting the state of modern-day child sex trafficking rings in a way that mirrored the parents and people in the story I just described. The countless victims that suffer horrific trauma as children, all of whose lives are forever changed. If society is going to say it has morals and integrity, its members must prove it with more than just talk. Such people deserve to be protected, even if those children are 60 years old now. Silence is compliance.

You Have to Want Help

I was able to connect Adam's bipolar sister with my Christian counselor, someone I knew could give her the kind of spiritual support she needed. If she wasn't going to go after her perpetrators, at least she could try to heal and learn to help others.

One of the things the counselor told her was to distance herself from her parents to begin the healing process. In fact, every mental health professional in every hospital she's been in since has also recommended the same thing. They're not only triggers for her, but also dysfunctional in their own right due to their own undiagnosed illnesses. What's more, they likely knew the three abusers.

Unfortunately, she refused to distance herself from them...ever. She still, to this day, lives right down the road, in constant contact. The little girl inside her could not make the break, (trauma bond) no matter how antagonistic or upsetting the relationship. In fact, little by little, the relationship seemed to make her sicker.

One night, she asked Adam and I to join her and her husband at a meeting with our counselor, where I sat in the waiting room and Adam joined his sister and her husband around a table in the adjoining kitchen. Within minutes, my husband burst into the room and said they needed me and that his sister was asking for me. I ran into the kitchen but didn't see her. Then I heard her crying out in the bathroom.

I found her curled up in a fetal position on the floor, screaming, *"No, Daddy! No, Daddy! Don't hurt me!"* She was rocking back and forth, her eyes dilated and black, just like her mother's we'd witnessed at times, as she continued to scream, *"No, Daddy,"* as if possessed by something demonic. Her family would have liked us to believe that was the truth and had suggested it numerous times. We all stood over her, uncertain of what to do next. I grabbed the counselor by the arm. *"This is so scary."* The counselor nodded. *"I know. I know."*

What were we to think? I knew Adam's father had been strict and mean. I also knew that he had beat them some because Adam had told me that he had suffered a couple of good beatings himself. His grandmother even had to stop one of the beatings he took as he recalls. But that particular night,

105
http://jocelynwreede.com/

we wondered if their father hadn't been guilty of something even more heinous. The way she had been acting and the things she had been saying during the 10-year old trance that caused us months of worry had us concerned that there may be more to it. Families with deep dark secrets are always hiding even more, so we would likely never know for sure.

Adam's sister had always been drop-dead gorgeous, capturing the attention of men wherever she went. Adam's father made it clear that he disapproved of the attention she got. For as long as Adam could remember, his father had told his sister, and whoever else would listen, that "pretty girls are just whores." I too had heard it many times after I entered what we called the "nest". Along with so much more.

There was so much pointing to more dysfunction and abuse than I'd imagined, but ultimately, neither Adam's sister nor her husband wanted to pursue the matter further. She even swore us to secrecy. Which for a time, we complied with. At one point, I was ready to schedule an inpatient-retreat in Tennessee where I knew she could get the help she needed away from everyone, but her husband put the kibosh on that. His reaction—and specifically his weakness that he showed through his willingness to allow his spouse to remain in a cycle of abuse—clued us in to that his own inner child was yet unhealed. To this day, he remains unwilling to do the hard to save her, refusing to man-up.

We couldn't let the matter rest, though. Adam's sister, by nature, had been a generous, caring Christian. I knew that if she sought to heal herself, she could, in turn, help others heal. Maybe if she understood that, it would inspire her to face the trauma in her life head-on.

At one point, I said to her,

"There are so many people hurting out there. So many people who have gone through or are going through what you've been through. Do you realize that if you grabbed a hold of your situation with both hands and did the mental, emotional, and spiritual work that you need to do, you could help so many people? If not for yourself, why not heal yourself to help others?"

She didn't respond. She didn't want to explore the trauma any further.

Even today, she cycles through episodes of mania and back to depression. She is often bedridden for weeks on end. Her "support system," as she likes to think of it, only enables her staying stuck on the cycle. This ongoing state of dysfunction results from her inability to be truthful with herself or anyone around her. And because of the people around her, she would take abuse for telling the truth, something we know about all too well.

THE VOICE INSIDE

As mentioned before, we refer to her habitat as "the nest," and it needs its secrets to stay buried if it is to go on propping up those who live in it. As long as no one finds out the truth, everyone can keep up the charade and simply point to Adam's sister as the "sick one," and blame her for everything, even though everyone around her is at least as sick as she is. Sickness that is apparent in everyone's unwillingness to stand up for truth and take the moral high ground by giving a voice to those little girls that didn't have a choice. Sadly, dysfunction breeds dysfunction, and only the strong break free.

Toxicity and dysfunction seek out more toxicity and dysfunction. Denial and keeping things hidden is necessary to the survival of a toxic environment. Making any other choice means facing the truth and doing the work of healing and growing. When toxicity grows instead, the damage is only exacerbated. For example, instead of increased healing, one of the many lies that continues to gain strength in order to deflect from facing the truth is that Adam's sister does it all for attention, that she's not even as ill as she portrays from all the trauma she suffered. The idea that so many people are willing to victimize her even more is beyond pathetic.

Anyone with even a basic understanding of mental illness would know that a sick person can't control their behaviors or moods. This is why we refer to such people as ill. But instead of properly caring for her, she has become a scapegoat and an object who is continually blamed so the toxicity and poison can spread. It is truly disgusting and sinful.

The truth is right there for everyone to acknowledge. It always has been. For 50 years. What about the parents that didn't call the authorities? Or take their little girls to the hospital? Or seek out psychological help for them? Blaming the victim is one thing, but this far down the line there is no excuse for perpetuating suffering like this. The villains who ruined so many lives are being protected because in this tragic scenario, they occupy the role of grandma and grandpa, mom and dad or friend. But regardless of their position in the family, they let the perpetrators go free all these years! How many more lives and families are they responsible for ruining as a result? And all just to save face, even at the expense of their own children and grandchildren's lives?

Where are the soldiers of God? Where are the strong men and women, the warriors who fight injustice and save the meek? We must rise up now to protect our children, no matter how old they may become.

Despite uncovering all the past secrets, lies, and abuse, what happened in the bathroom that night was shoved under the rug and never revisited again as everything always was. I could never forget it, though. Neither could Adam. As a result, we became outcasts from the family by choice. We couldn't pretend or hide the lies like all the others seem to easily do. Integrity. We refuse to surround ourselves with anything damaging and fake like that, that doesn't align with our core values and convictions. I keep notes with me in my phone as written, non-negotiables, core values, and I carry them with me everywhere.

When Adam's sister attempted to hang herself not long ago, her enabling, weak partner blamed Adam, who had just come home from a near death experience of his own after a battle with double covid pneumonia. With no real healing or truth in sight, and no attempt at finding the correct treatment, we were forced to cut contact with his sister and her husband as well.

Owning Up

The cycles of trauma and chaos would continue in my husband's family without our participation. The two of us would make sure of that. There was no way we would allow the manipulations and toxicity to continue into our own son. If they weren't willing to examine the cycle of abuse in which they were active participants, our only line of defense was to save ourselves. The only way to a happy, healthy life of abundance was to rid ourselves of the unhappy, unhealthy relationships in our lives. We cut off all contact to break the generational cycle.

Honestly, I don't feel hatred toward my husband's family. Thoughts of them give me the creeps and disgust, knowing all we know now. But I don't harbor any bitterness or anger because the most important lesson God taught me over the years was letting bitterness go. For ME. For my own family. For my own divine destiny. I would never suggest that the path is short or easy, but I really feel nothing for them. We all must make choices and decisions in life. We made ours, and they definitely made theirs.

By contrast, when you give in to bitterness, you generate a negative forcefield that repels positive energy. And once you let it go, you make yourself available to accept the right people into your life, the people who will support and uplift you. You need to grow you in a positive and healthy way. Growth is supposed to happen, so you can achieve the heights of awesomeness you have the right to become. The coaches, mentors, and mental health professionals we have worked with have guided us this far, and we never intend to stop learning and growing.

Likewise, when dealing with trauma. Unless you have the will and the strength to look deep within yourself and do the work that needs to be done, trauma will define the rest of your life. If you don't do the work, you're wasting your existence on this earth. You also risk continuing those unhealthy cycles by passing them on to your own children. It matters who you choose to surround your children with. Parents owe it to their children to be healthy and to educate themselves. This is the cycle you should pass on.

THE VOICE INSIDE

Remember that no matter who you are, you can be so much better. You can have better relationships, better careers, and a better understanding of your place in this world.

Be your own detective in your life. See how the dots connect. Be the one who breaks the cycle of generational neglect, trauma, and abuse, even if it makes you the enemy. You WILL be viewed as the enemy by those who are unwilling to explore, anyway. I know this because I was the enemy of my stepchildren and in-laws. Become THE ONE, the complete badass that puts an END to the unhealthy cycle FOREVER. Fortunately, my stepdaughter was strong enough to dig through the bs and lies and willing to alter her perspective, for which we remain eternally grateful.

We've built such an extremely loving, genuine relationship with her, the chains are broken and all that weight we all once felt is gone. It's so rewarding to watch her mind flourish after SOOO many years of wrong information being pounded into it by people she thought loved her but were more interested in their own agendas than what was happening to her inside. Manipulation is not love.

It's up to you to "wake up" and break the curse of generational abuse and trauma. You don't have to look at life through the lens of someone else's messed-up history. As long as you never stop learning and growing on this side of Heaven, you can always do better. So, make the decision to be better. Don't settle for whatever hand you may have been dealt. Healthy people do exist—I know because I have found them.

"Healing generational trauma takes courage and strength. It's common for dysfunctional families to deny their abuse. They silence victims and dump toxic shame onto them. Complicit families keep abuse alive from generation to generation until one brave survivor boldly ends the cycle of abuse."

Dana Arcuri

I had broken cycles of abuse and tried to intervene in the name of God. Sometimes my help was welcome and sometimes I was reviled for my stance. It didn't matter. I had heard His words. But was I done being tested?

Takeaway

- Personal growth is vital in breaking the cycles of generational trauma and abuse.
- Sometimes you are tasked with recognizing dysfunction in a family or relationship, even if no one else recognizes it. Then it is up to you to take positive action.

THE VOICE INSIDE

- Don't let fear get in the way of halting a cycle of abuse, especially if you have a family or plan to have a family. Now is the time.
- If you're part of a cycle of abuse, you're either living in accordance with it, or you are the one to break it.
- Trauma is never-ending unless it is resolved. Full stop.
- Prepare for the inevitability if you want to change for the better but those around you do not. You will have to be stronger than them. And for that strength, you may sometimes feel like an outcast. In reality, it's only because you have become who God intended you to be. Standing in his truth is the only way.
- Toxic people breed toxicity. Stay away from them.
- 99% of people don't actually want the truth. They want the lies/perception they have grown comfortable with. Join the 1% who have what it takes.

Chapter 6

Balls To the Wall

"No matter how many times you get knocked down, keep getting back up. God sees your resolve. He sees your determination. And when you do everything, you can do, that's when God will step in and do what you can't do."

Joel Osteen

There's no way I can write my story without addressing 2021; the year Covid came to our house. If there ever was a lesson God wanted to drive home, it came with the pandemic.

Covid reminded us that, for all our strengths and dynamics and intellect and ideas, we humans are a fragile species. We are only here for a short while, so it is important to remember that every day of our lives.

THE VOICE INSIDE

"The life of mortals is like grass; they flourish like a flower of the field; the wind blows over it and it is gone, and its place remembers it no more."

So, it is written in Psalm 103: 15-16 (Feel free to substitute "Covid-19" for "wind").

We can and must make each day count and make changes in our lives when needed. We have the capacity to educate ourselves, to alter our surroundings as well as the neural pathways in our brain, and to love whomever we wish. We can control what we eat, where we travel, and whom we befriend. We have so many choices in the United States and so many freedoms, but when Covid hit, the faith of many was tested.

My own faith was the fundamental principle for me in combatting fear. There wasn't a thing I took for granted during that time when so many were succumbing to sickness and death, especially my connection to Jesus. I prayed daily. Boy, did I pray daily. I knew that God was never far, but He definitely tested me, as He did everyone else. The point was—and remains—never to lose faith ... or hope.

"Darkness comes. In the middle of it, the future looks blank. The temptation to quit is huge. Don't. You are in good company… You will argue with yourself that there is no way forward. But with God, nothing is impossible. He has more ropes and ladders and tunnels out of pits than you can conceive. Wait. Pray without ceasing. Hope."

John Piper, American New Testament scholar, and Baptist theologian

No One Is Immune

In September 2021, there was a clue we were beginning to crawl out of the ditch that was Covid-19. Like so many others, Adam, our son, and I were itching to get back to some semblance of normalcy. The county fair rolled around again in early fall, and we thought it might give us a chance to get back into the swing of things.

It was a beautiful, warm, sunny day. The fair was packed with people that seemed as eager as we were to partake in the food trucks and festivities. The mood was positive, the chili cheese fries and barbeque tasted better than I remembered, and every color and smell seemed more vivid than ever. Suffice it to say, we were happy just to be back in the land of the living.

THE VOICE INSIDE

Two days later, I felt sicker than I had ever felt in my life. I woke with a temperature of 103, my head throbbing as though I'd been on a bender the night before—I remembered what those were like, and I had vowed never to experience one again. I hauled myself out of bed, determined to muscle through the day, but I didn't have a spare bone capable of supporting my aching body. I wasn't fooling anyone, least of all myself.

Finally, I told Adam that I needed to go to the hospital. *"Don't worry,"* he said in the car ride there.
"You don't have Covid. It's just the flu."

The hospital was closed to everyone that was suspected of having Covid, so I waited in the vehicle. When it was my turn, I asked the nurse if she would please give me the PCR test instead of the rapid test. I felt sure I had Covid, and I didn't want to take the chance of a rapid test showing a false negative.
We rushed home afterward, but I could barely put one foot in front of the other to the front door.

"Stay away from me," I called to our son as I maneuvered my way to my bedroom.

Within twenty-four hours, I knew for sure I had Covid. Adam had to go to work the following day, so he set me up with some food, water, and meds before leaving. He did the same the next day and the next. Now, Adam is a big, burly outdoorsman kind of guy, always on the go, never one to complain, but each night, he looked paler and more stooped than the next.

"I'm okay," he said to me to preempt my concern. *"I'm okay. I'm not going to get it. I'm not going to get it."*

That was his mantra until he came home from work at the end of the week, stripped down to his underwear, climbed into bed with me, and slept for three days straight. Our poor son was literally throwing food, thermometers, and bottles of water at us from the doorway because I forbade him to come into our room.

"I do not want you to get sick! You can't get sick; do you hear me?" I wheezed at him.

By the eleventh day, I was still looking and feeling like a wet rag, but Adam looked even worse. His skin color had gone from pale to gray.

I grabbed the pulsometer—that neat little device that reads blood oxygen levels and pulse—off the dresser and clamped it on his finger. It read 82, a terrible reading (a level of 92 percent or lower is a possible indicator of hypoxemia, a seriously low level of oxygen in the blood).

I turned to my husband and said, *"Do not argue with me. You need to get up. We are going to the hospital."*
When he didn't argue, I knew we were in trouble.

From Hands Raised Hope Springs

They gave Adam oxygen as soon as he got to the hospital. The hospital staff told us he would have to stay. I couldn't remain with him because they were putting him in isolation. I returned home to be with our twelve-year-old son. There was nothing else I could do. I cried all the way home, but knew I had to get back. I worried how my son would react when he saw that I had returned without his dad.

My son and I Facetimed with Adam, but it was frightening seeing him, weak and listless, in a full BIPAP oxygen mask. No one was allowed to visit, not even the closest of kin. People were dying right and left of him. Patients who had been in the same oxygen masks as Adam one day were dead the next. Facebook was full of mothers, fathers, sons, and daughters talking to their loved ones via Facetime in sterile, white hospital rooms.

I was so worried that I couldn't eat or even sleep in our bed without him. Sometimes I'd lay out on the area rug in our living room just for a change of pace. Of course, our son got Covid, despite my best precautions. Though I was still feeling weak, I needed to care for him now.

Twenty-four days later, Adam got out of isolation. But this was an improvement over only a few days earlier. I had received a 5:00 a.m. phone call. No one gets a call at 5:00 a.m. with good news. I was scared even to answer the phone. When I did, it was one of my husband's nurses.

"I wanted to call and let you know that there are doctors and nurses in your husband's room right now. They're going to put him on a ventilator because he's maxed out on oxygen and dropping."

My heart just sank. I felt like everything inside me had been sucked out of my body. My mom would later tell me that I had called her at just after 5:00 a.m. in hysterics. According to her, the only word I could say was, "Come." To this day, I don't remember talking to her. Gavin and I had been huddled together in our house for two solid weeks. The only people we saw were my mother and friends of ours dropping off food and medicine on our porch. We needed support.

I do remember that my mother stayed with us for a while to care for me and Gavin. I had to try to get it together, if not for myself, at least for my son.

That Saturday, Adam was fighting for his life. I stepped out into the front yard barefoot, hoping to try to ground myself and get some fresh air. I hadn't gone ten feet when I dropped to my knees, as though some force of gravity had come down on me.

Hands raised in the air, sobbing, I started praying—hardcore praying, crying aloud and to the heavens. I prayed to God not to take Adam. *How was I going to raise our son by myself?* I asked. *How would I tell him that Daddy wasn't ever coming home?* My praying lasted until I exhausted myself, at which point I pitched forward, facedown into the grass, wrung dry. I had no more tears to cry. I didn't even think about the people driving by who doubtlessly wondered what I was doing.

Who Needs the Answer, Receives

I wouldn't learn until the next day that, while I had been on my front lawn, praying to God—and unsure whether He was listening—my husband had been summoning all the fight in him, despite being maxed out of oxygen.

He had told the doctors and nurses standing over him,

"Get the hell out of this room. Just get out. If I'm going to die, I'm going to die on my own. I am not getting on that ventilator."

They couldn't put him on the ventilator if he was going to fight them, which he continued to do as his temperature soared over 104.

"I'm going home," he'd insisted.

Though Adam was a Christian who believed in God, worshipping in church alongside me, he had never had the personal experiences with God that I'd had. But that day in the hospital, running out of fight, he told me that God spoke to him directly.

"You're going to be fine," were the words he'd heard. *"You're going to make it. You're going to make it out of here."*

Adam said he dozed off, tossing and turning in a kind of twilight sleep, at least in the knowledge that he would eventually walk out of the hospital and return home. Forty-eight days later, he did precisely that. Two days before Gavin turned 13 and still dependent on oxygen, he came home. Satan had spoken to Adam during his struggle, telling him *to*

tear off the mask and oxygen and walk out the door.
Thankfully, Adam listened to the voice of God instead.

It was another one of life's pivots. We both felt changed. We felt fueled and hopeful for the future. Adam had nearly died, but now he was home. If there were any dreams that we were putting off pursuing because we thought we had all the time in the world, it was time to move those dreams front and center. It was balls to the wall.

A Reminder

God doesn't remind me of His word with a whisper. Instead, He seems to do it with a bullhorn. Repeatedly, He has reinforced my belief that it is in the most challenging times of my life that I gain the most clarity about my values and my direction. When I'm in the mindset of seeking direct comfort from Him, I create an internal environment to receive His messages. Although I can't understand why God speaks to me or anyone else when He does, I do know that He answers me when I am most in need. God's timing is perfect.

"And he said, 'Go out and stand on the mount before the Lord.' And behold, the Lord passed by, and a great and strong wind tore the mountains and broke in pieces the rocks before the Lord, but the Lord was not in the wind. And after the wind an earthquake, but the Lord was not in the earthquake. And

124

after the earthquake a fire, but the Lord was not in the fire. And after the fire the sound of a low whisper. And when Elijah heard it, he wrapped his face in his cloak and went out and stood at the entrance of the cave. And behold, there came a voice to him and said, 'What are you doing here, Elijah?'"

1 Kings 19:11-13 ESV

God has answered me more times than I could ever have hoped for in an entire lifetime—directly, indirectly, and by putting certain people in my path. Some of those people have become family, some friends, and some are the most important mentors I could ask for.

Takeaway

- Make each day count because we have no idea what God has in store for us tomorrow.
- Don't put off until tomorrow that which you should start today. That may sound like an oversimplification, but after experiencing a world shut down by Covid, you ought to know better.
- Faith in God is like an immunization, not a cure. Don't wait until trying times to put your faith in God.

THE VOICE INSIDE

- Ask God for help. If you have faith, you will receive His help in one form or another.

Chapter 7

Find Your People and Your Purpose

"I got a shot at life. A higher power loved me enough to put me here, and I have to take advantage of this human experience. People who don't know me might see me coming down the street and feel sorry for me. I don't need—or want—that pity. I want them to see themselves and look inward at the things that are <u>holding them back</u>. As Eminem aptly says, we only get one shot, and <u>our mindset about that opportunity</u> can be more crippling than any syndrome. Are you taking your shot?"

One of my coaches-
Nick Santonastasso

THE VOICE INSIDE

I have been fortunate to find many mentors in my life who have helped provide me with community and support along my journey. One of them, Nick Santonastasso, an author, motivational speaker, bodybuilder, and coach, was born with a rare condition called Hanhart Syndrome, which left him without legs and one arm. He lives his life with purpose and vision, and joy. Part of the reason he can do that is because he believes his vulnerability is one of his greatest strengths. He has said that he doesn't have the luxury of masking his vulnerabilities; they are physically front and center. As a leader and motivational speaker, he encourages people to show themselves, warts and all, and embrace their own vulnerability and humanity.

For as long as I can remember, I imagined vulnerability as one of my superpowers. I've never been one to hide my feelings, my opinions, my battle scars, or the trauma in my life. Instead, I was meant to help bring people out of the darkness by showing myself up as an example. By transcending my pain, I imagined I could give hope and guidance to others to do the same. If I could turn my life around, so could others. After all, our mistakes are the most significant things that can happen to us. They are the only means by which we learn. Our struggles—the messes of our lives—are our lessons and messages.

My mess is my message, the lessons I have to offer people. When I started to share my life story, including the darkest, most hurtful days of my life, I saw how it helped others to share their stories. I owed it to myself to heal and set myself free to help others do the same.

Once God entered the equation, it became my moral obligation to help others. I felt my soul calm, and my head become clearer. Everything that had happened to me was for a reason. God did not let me suffer if it wasn't for a purpose— to tell my truth and share my message.

For years, I begged God to please take away the abuse and the pain. From my vantage point, I thought He was ignoring me. *Why wouldn't He take it away? Why did I have to go through all that I was going through?* At times, I grew angry with Him. *Why did I have to suffer?* And finally, I saw that all that pain and abuse—the mess of my life—would provide hope for others.

When I received baptism in the Mohican River, I began to find clarity about my life, and in clarity, I was able to process the pain in my life. That was an important milestone in my life—a pivot. I dreamed of one day being able to baptize others, to help others see the light and begin their own transformations. I wanted to help those men and women who were still drinking to mask their pain, as I had once done. What were they running away from? Their partners, their loneliness, their very existence?

An Equal-Opportunity Lender

The thing about pain is that it's an equal-opportunity lender. It doesn't care whether you're rich or poor, black, or white, male or female. It comes for all of us.

I remember someone I knew, a guy I used to see at a neighborhood bar quite often when I was drinking. He was a successful lawyer—a district attorney, in fact—with a nice home, a new car, and a family, yet any lunch hour I hit the bar, I saw him there on a barstool, drinking his same liquid lunch. I look back now and can't help but wonder what he was running from.

Pain is miserable, but it can actually help move the needle to the side of recovery. When you become so sick and tired of being sick and tired, sometimes you are forced to find a way out. Enough is enough. That was the way for me. I had to hit rock bottom for the needle to start moving in the opposite direction—to begin moving forward. For some people, it's easier to remain stuck and pass the blame: my father, mother, sister, wife, or husband is to blame for my unhappiness and my mess. But those who cannot move past their pain and blame will probably be miserable for their entire lives, and I can't think of anything sadder than that.

It's hard to do the work, to look inside, to change, to seek help, and to accept that there is a power greater than oneself, especially when one is experiencing some dark days.

However, those darkest days can show you what you need to know about yourself, just as Carl Jung said, "That which we need the most will be found where we least want to look."

 Anyone can be happy, positive, and inspired when things are going well, but when everything seems to be falling apart, that is the time to focus on hope. Hope is the light at the end of the tunnel, however far away that light might appear, it is there. And in that hope is the time to find faith, to seek support, and to look within oneself. Keep on. Hope will put you on the journey to the light at the tunnel's end, but you have to do the work to reach that light successfully.

 There's a great story by the thirteenth century Sufi metaphysician and author Rumi about going beyond one's comfort zone and doing the difficult work in the way that Jung describes.

 According to the story, a drunk is looking for the keys he lost in a dark alley. He crawls around on his hands and knees, frantically searching, when a passerby notices the drunk's search and stops to help. Together, they search for the keys under the streetlamp, the only light source in the alley.

After a long while of unsuccessful searching, the passerby asks the drunk, *"Are you sure you dropped your keys here?"* *"No, I dropped them over there,"* he replies, pointing off into the distance.

Confused, the passerby asks, *"If you dropped your keys in the dark alley, then why are you looking for them here?"* *"Because the light is better here under the streetlight, and I can see more clearly."*

That pretty much sums up the human condition. We tend to search for answers and meaning in the wrong places. In a spiritual sense, we need to explore the dark depths of our being and examine what is difficult. We need to find ourselves, our faith, our God, and the people we want to be in our lives.

Finding My Person

While I was drinking and in despair, it was like being on a road trip down a narrow highway with no headlights. At times, that was quite literally the case. When I met Adam, it was as though the brights of those headlights came on.

The significance of meeting my life partner has never been lost on me. I fell for Adam early on but watching him every other weekend with his children was the clincher. Never having known a father's love for his child, I was floored by Adam's love and devotion to his children. I knew for sure that he was my dude.

Through the years, Adam has always supported me, even if he didn't always agree with me or necessarily have the same vision. If I'm passionate about a belief or an ideal, he is right there, pushing me to pursue it. With all I've been through, having him by my side has been a literal Godsend. And honestly, it has not only been essential to have Adam's support on my journey of personal development, but it has also been fun and exciting. Together, we celebrate our successes and mourn our losses. We exchange ideas and buoy each other's faith.

It's not easy to pursue your dreams and your right and truthful path, but it's even more difficult when you don't have a partner who supports you. It's like being with someone who doesn't speak the same language.

I vividly remember meeting a very devout Christian woman in Celebrate Recovery who happened to be married to an atheist. As an adult, that woman's husband had the freedom of choice, no doubt, but the woman was miserable that her husband's spiritual beliefs were so diametrically opposed to hers. It soon became apparent that the union would not work.

Finding My People

I knew I was put here to help people. Help them to heal from abuse, to excavate the purpose and meaning in their lives, to help them find their truths. I knew I could do that by sharing my faith and exposing my messy, humbling past.

THE VOICE INSIDE

Once I found a loving, supportive partner, I was able to find my tribe—the people who are on the same journey as me. On life's road trip, it's like having a family with me, the kind of family who supports and encourages my trip. Once I realized my purpose, I was able to attract that tribe.

So many people live their lives on autopilot, doing the same unsatisfying job forty hours or more a week, year after year. They numb themselves with alcohol, drugs, or other vices and find themselves in frustrating and loveless or unhealthy relationships. They refuse to reach out for help because they're scared of looking weak when, in fact, the ability to reach out for help is a sign of strength. They remain stuck because they don't progress in their work or spiritual life, so they attract others like them. I know those people because I was once on the same path. I also know how difficult it is to change paths, to choose the journey into the light.

I love the anecdote that one of my mentors told me about the behavior of crabs trapped in a bucket: Though any one crab can easily start to escape, the group will pull it back in the bucket to ensure the demise of the whole group. It is the same for certain groups of humans—out of envy or resentment, members of a group will try to stifle the progress and self-confidence of any member who achieves success independently of the others.

Like anything worthwhile, it required a ton of work and a lot of soul-searching to pull away from people who didn't have my best interests at heart. But I knew that if I put in the effort, I would not only find my tribe but would also find the platform to teach my life's lessons. I searched and searched, and once God spoke to me, my search became more definitive and less confusing. I prayed to God to please point me in the right direction.

Believing I was meant to be a Christian life coach, I attended a Christian Coaching School. I earned my ICF certificate, but something was missing. I believed I was destined to open a ministry, especially because I had received so many signs and confirmations from God. I felt like that was how God wanted me to find my tribe to teach my life's lessons. But more signs from Him convinced me that wasn't how I would find my tribe, either.

I didn't give up because I knew what I wanted. Like always, God had a plan for me all along. I didn't realize that the plan included the internet, where I found people who loved and understood who I was and what I had to offer. In finding them, I also found a built-in community, the tribe I'd been searching for.

From my coach Keaton Hoskins:

"I wish I could convince everyone of their real value and ability in this life. I wish I could change their thoughts from mediocre to superhuman. I wish I could convince you to see yourself as God sees you in all your potential and power. I wish I could convince you to live the damn life you were born to live, to convince you what you're truly an heir to. I don't know how long I'll be on this earth, but I do know I want to spend the rest of my days convincing this to those I come in contact with. I'll give every ounce of energy and time to this cause. No one was born to come here and live in mediocrity but to be heirs of fucking power beyond measure. I'll spend the rest of my days teaching, preaching, and educating this ideology. I won't stop because I believe it to my core, to my soul."

My Purpose

Whatever God has given you is specific to who you are and what you need. You just have to find that tiny seed inside of you. Everyone has their own path and their own seed. It is not the same for me as it is for the next person, yet we are all the same, all deserving of His guidance, love, and community. The more in tune you become with Him, the stronger your purpose becomes.

When I wake up in the morning, I know that God is with me. It's as though I have my absolute best friend sitting on my shoulder. We converse all day long, as in the most intimate of relationships. But God can speak to anyone who knows how to listen to Him. You just need to be patient because it may require a degree of waiting, and boy, people hate to wait for things. Waiting is one of the hardest things we are asked to do in life, but if you're willing to pray and to listen, really listen, you will find Him trying to get your attention.

Don't think that whatever happened to you in the past, or whatever bad thing you may have done, will preclude God's answers to your prayers. Don't let society or your friends or family tell you otherwise. You have a purpose; if you find your faith, you will find your purpose.

I wasn't always aware of my purpose, though I always knew how to lead. In school, I never let myself get pigeonholed. I could run with the "popular" kids, the jocks, the outcasts—anyone on the fringe—because I made my direction in life. Though I hadn't yet had a purpose, I always knew that I could do big things—by helping others realize their potential, working with inspiring leaders and mentors, writing a book, and making a difference in the world.

To live without purpose is to live in darkness. It is to live an aimless, meaningless life without knowing your *target*, so to speak. Interestingly, the word "sin" comes from an archery term meaning to miss the mark—the target. If you missed the mark, then you sinned. Maybe our sins have to do with missing our marks in life, in proceeding without purpose. I would tend to believe that.

My life unraveled when I tried to find my purpose without knowing God. But when I plugged God into my life and committed to living in accordance with the Scripture, everything started to make sense, including my purpose. Since then, I have been able to help others to see that if they do the same, they, too, can find their purpose.

About eight years ago, I started having the same dream over and over, night after night. In the dream, I was on a stage, speaking to a crowd. I still suffered from panic attacks at that point, so I couldn't make heads or tails about what the dream meant. I didn't want to get on a stage. Hell no! But then I realized that God was telling me to find a way to tell my story and show others what I have found. So, I listened to Him.

I have told my story and will continue to tell it because it can change people's lives. In telling my truth, the whole messy truth, and the story of my own redemption, I have been able to help others transform their lives. I have seen my story bring people to tears because they recognize it in themselves. When that happens, I know I have hit my mark.

He Knows Better

God wants you to have the best life possible, but you need to show up and do the work or, as I like to think, follow God's simple directions. We are all meant for greatness because we are all born in the image of God. Be proud of who you are. I believe that when we are honest with each other and tell our life stories without shame and embarrassment, we inspire others to do the same. And when we tell our stories and embrace who we are, we can begin to pursue our dreams, our purpose.

God designed this world for us, and in that design lies our happiness, as well as our troubles and traumas, but those troubles and traumas teach us how to navigate life. We need to experience them in order to learn and to find our purpose and happiness. God knows life isn't easy and that we, His children, can be pissed off with our friends and family and life in general. Sometimes we find ourselves pissed off with Him in our misdirected anger and frustration, especially in times of darkness and tragedy. But He can take it. God has broad shoulders. He understands that anger is a natural response for us when things feel out of our control, or when we don't get what we want, or when something terrible happens.

Ultimately, we must trust that God is full of love and grace. Everything that happens to us is designed by Him. He oversees all situations, despite our conceit of thinking we control things.

There's a song from the 2000 animated children's movie, *Joseph: King of Dreams,* that beautifully encapsulates the question of anger toward God. It is sung by Joseph when he is despairing and ready to give up on his faith after being sold into slavery.

In the song "You Know Better Than I," Joseph decides to trust in Him, even though his situation is dire:

> *I thought I did what's right*
> *I thought I had the answers*
> *I thought I chose the surest road*
> *But that road brought me here*
>
> *So, I put up a fight*
> *And told you how to help me*
> *Now just when I have given up*
> *The truth is coming clear*
>
> *You know better than I*
> *You know the way*
> *I've let go the need to know why*
> *For You know better than I*

JOCELYN WREEDE

If this has been a test
I cannot see the reason
But maybe knowing "I don't know"
Is part of getting through

I tried to do what's best
But faith has made it easy
To see the best thing I can do
Is to put my trust in You

For You know better than I
You know the way
I've let go the need to know why
For You know better than I

I saw one cloud and thought it was a sky
I saw a bird and thought that I could follow
But it was You who taught that bird to fly
If I let You reach me
Will You teach me?

For You know better than I
You know the way
I've let go the need to know why
I'll take what answers You supply
You know better than I

141

Takeaway

- We can all better ourselves in one way or another. If you can, don't wait until you're at rock bottom to do the work.
- There is no way of avoiding pain in this life. In one way or another, to larger and smaller degrees, pain always seems to be around the corner, so fortify yourself with your faith and trust in God.
- Reach out to people who can help you better your life. Open your heart to love and let go of the people in your life who seem to pull you down.
- We are all put here for a purpose. Find your purpose, your reason for being here. You will be awed at how your life is made better through your efforts.

Chapter 8

The Mess of It

"Don't worry about anything; instead, pray about everything.
Tell God what you need and thank him for all he has done.
Then you will experience God's peace, which exceeds
anything we can understand. His peace will guard your hearts
and minds as you live in Christ Jesus."

Philippians 4:6-7 (New Living Translation)

After the dissolution of my first marriage, I hit the darkest, most despairing time of my life, the one time in my life when I imagined that leaving this physical world would be the only answer to my pain. What I later realized, as crazy as it may sound, was that hitting rock bottom was the greatest gift from God. It allowed me to rebuild my entire life in the right way—the way of God. I felt like the mythical immortal phoenix that dies in a burst of flames only to gain new life from its ashes.

Overcome, Don't Run

The person I used to be was built by my surroundings—the influences, people, places, and things I had little control over as a child. Whether we like it or not, and whether we're aware of it, we are taught directly and indirectly by our parents about money, emotional intelligence, and relationships. If you had fearful parents, chances are you will be fearful. If your parents possessed a scarcity mindset, the same will be passed on to you. If your parents had unhealthy habits, you are likely to develop unhealthy habits, too, unless you take action to change the course of your life.

If your parents simply accepted their lot in life, no matter how bad or stressful, you will most likely do the same. And, especially if your parents were abusive, surrounded you with unhealthy people, or they were survivors of abuse, and that's all you experienced as a child, you are more likely to wind up in an abusive relationship or develop abusive behavior patterns.

But it doesn't have to be that way. You can overcome your childhood if you're willing to put it under a microscope. If you're willing to examine those original negative thoughts and habits handed down from your parents, and the people who influenced you when you were a child, you can forge a new path. You can accomplish so much if you're willing to overcome your obstacles.

Sure, you can try to run and hide. You may last a long while running from your truth and eschewing God for more immediate gratification. You can delay facing your fears and insecurities by numbing yourself with drugs or alcohol, or sex, but that will ultimately make your station in life—*your* situation—worse.

I see you. I am you. I know how hard it is to switch from autopilot to a life of introspection and purpose. But no matter where you are in your life, there are two ways to go—downhill (even further than you may already be) or about-face.

I know what it's like to hit bottom. In fact, I was so down on myself and life that I seemed to be looking for ways to make my situation even worse. I wanted even more pain, to punish myself even more.

When I became clear about my life, about healing, and about God, I realized how many opportunities awaited me. I didn't have to live in the past. I didn't have to react to life in the ways I had been conditioned to react. I could change my reactions, change my perception, change my outlook, and change my relationships to ones with healthy individuals. Once I became more intentional in my faith in God and started reaching out to others for help and talking about my pain, I realized I had choices. The more I shared my story and pain, the less power it had over me, and the more it opened me up to meeting influential, like-minded people. I no longer needed the distractions I once had relied on.

Stuck No More

There's a beautiful Zen story about getting stuck in certain habits and ways of thinking, and how anger, in particular, can keep us from moving forward in our lives. You may know it because there are a lot of versions of the story out there, but the one I recall is from a children's picture book called *Zen Shorts* by Jon J. Muth.

"Two traveling monks reached a town where there was a young woman waiting to step out of her sedan chair. The rains had made deep puddles, and she couldn't step across without spoiling her silken robes. She stood there, looking very cross and impatient. She was scolding her attendants. They had nowhere to place the packages they held for her, so they couldn't help her across the puddle.

The younger monk noticed the woman, said nothing, and walked by. The older monk quickly picked her up and put her on his back, transported her across the water, and put her down on the other side. She didn't thank the older monk; she just shoved him out of the way and departed.

As they continued on their way, the young monk was brooding and preoccupied. After several hours, unable to hold his silence, he spoke out.

"That woman back there was very selfish and rude, but you picked her up on your back and carried her! Then she didn't even thank you!"

"I set the woman down hours ago," the older monk replied. "Why are you still carrying her?"

No doubt, I was once stuck. So many negative things had taken a hold of my life, including family and friends who had no interest in seeing me become unstuck.

The people around you may feel threatened because you are taking steps to better yourself. They may want to blame you for everything in their lives. But it's usually because you are drawing attention to their own shortcomings and forcing them to confront their own failure to act. Once you fix your faith and your mind and your body, you become a reminder of all that is wrong in their lives. You become a pariah (outcast). So be it. But there's always a chance you become a beacon for them in their darkness. Whatever the case, you must proceed on your journey whether people want to join you or not.

The recovery process isn't a straightforward path. It often involves three steps forward and two steps back, sometimes one step forward and two back, but the addition of God in your life can make that process just a hair smoother. God gave me the strength to find love, to find people who would help lift me up and nourish me, and to find purpose. God led me to understand that the mess of my life would become the message I was meant to share with others in the hopes of setting them on a path toward the light.

Finding Meaning in the Mess

The essence of my mess equaling my message is this: embracing and finding meaning in life's messiness can lead you to personal transformation and a deeper understanding of yourself and the world around you.

To do that, you must:

1. Embrace your struggles. Life's challenges and struggles can be disheartening and overwhelming. However, rather than avoiding or resenting them, you can choose to embrace them as opportunities for growth. Just as a seed must break through the

darkness and dirt to sprout and bloom, your personal growth often arises from navigating through the messy and challenging times of your life. The mess becomes the canvas on which to paint your stories of resilience and strength.

2. Learn from your failures. Failure is an integral part of 'the human' experience. We all stumble, make mistakes, and face disappointments. Yet, within the ashes of failure lies invaluable wisdom. Each setback teaches us valuable lessons, motivates us to reassess our approach, and builds resilience. We learn to persevere, adapt, and ultimately achieve our goals through failure. Our mess-ups become steppingstones toward success.

3. Build empathy and compassion. Life's messy moments shape us individually and deepen our understanding and empathy for others. When we experience pain, loss, or struggle, we develop a greater capacity to empathize with others facing similar challenges. Our own mess becomes the bridge that connects us to the shared human experience, fostering compassion and a desire to help others on their own journeys.

4. Find meaning and purpose. Often, it is during the most challenging times that we gain clarity about our passions and purpose. When faced with adversity, we are forced to evaluate what truly matters to us. The

mess becomes an opportunity to reevaluate our choices, redefine our priorities, and align our lives with our deepest aspirations. Through introspection and reflection, we can discover a sense of purpose that guides us forward, even in the face of uncertainty.

5. Inspire others. As you navigate your own messy journeys, you have the power to inspire and uplift others. Sharing your stories of triumph over adversity provides hope and encouragement to those who may be facing similar struggles. Your mess becomes a message of resilience, inspiring others to persevere, overcome their challenges, and embrace their own messy paths.

I challenge you to find the path you deserve to be on and to find faith in building a better and more resilient life filled with love and success. It is what I want for you and, more importantly, it is what God wants for you, as well.

Takeaway

- Our earliest teachers are our parents, for better or for worse. That does not mean that their lessons have to be the most important or the longest lasting.

- You may run from your troubles or misguided living, but you can't hide, at least not forever.
- The recovery process is long and arduous, but anything worthwhile in life is not easy.
- Your struggles are the messes that lead to your success in life.
- Failure is the only way we learn our lessons. Our wins may be incredible, but our failures are indelibly etched in our brains so that we may try to avoid the same ones.
- Through your messes and struggles, you may best learn compassion and empathy.
- Find what matters most to you in life. Use that as the purpose of your existence.
- Share your mess and your failures as quickly as you do your successes. You will inspire others with your truth.

Conclusion

It took nearly half my life to harness the immense strength I had within me. It was always there, but God had a long, arduous journey planned for me before I fully realized that strength. He had to push me out of my comfort zone and force me to face my fears and vulnerabilities. My life truly felt like a trial by fire, but now I'm comforted in the understanding that I am part of a great tribe of people who have felt as I have.

I believe that we all face trials in our life. God does not prevent those trials from happening, no matter how faithful and steadfast you may be, so I don't want you to be under the false understanding that belief in Jesus will protect you from life's pitfalls. God will test your faith, no matter how strong it is and no matter how righteous your path is. He wants to remind you that, no matter how much control you think you have in your life, the reality is that God is the One in control. He is the only one able to see the grand design, while we view fragments of the whole.

Once I understood all that, not only did my personal and spiritual life fall into place, but I was also able to integrate my faith around building financially successful businesses that felt intuitive and meaningful. My spiritual practices led me to build trust with clients, customers, and partners, which only made those business relationships more meaningful and fulfilling. One might not equate financial concerns with Christian faith, but there happens to be endless biblical principles applicable to financial stewardship.

Coaching other people has allowed me to understand the value of taking risks and the importance of consciously acquiring debt, all balanced by building a strong network of friends. In business, as in my personal life, I reach out for guidance, when necessary, in the form of my mentors and my network. Now when I form business relationships, my focus is on creating a positive work environment that fosters personal growth. For me, that growth is always a reflection of my faith.

Although I believe in my Christian faith and speak regularly to God, not everyone in my life needs to share my views on spirituality. My huge network of like-minded people makes it possible for me to face the challenges of personal development and business growth more easily. I finally found my tribe. And although I attribute my successes to my faith, that does not mean that I preach everywhere and to everyone.

Not everyone is ready to bring Jesus into their life. I respect that. I respect all denominations of faith and all the unique ways we humans find strength to carry on. There is beauty and value in the many ways we choose to worship and find spiritual fulfillment.

THE VOICE INSIDE

I can only tell you my story and how Jesus swelled my heart to help anyone in need and to help me develop understanding and personal success. I can only tell you that Jesus has helped me to meet my trials and tribulations head-on. He is my hope, my comfort, and my inspiration. Ultimately, that is the real message I want to share with you. People good and bad may have *"made me",* but HE was the artist. You can be Lost but always be Found.

I wish you success in your effort to heal from abuse and to break generational cycles of abuse in your personal life. If hearing my message and my story has made you curious about how to proceed in your relationship with Jesus, if you need support or guidance in any of the areas I shared about, I am open to hearing from you.

Contact Page

Watch This Site: www.JocelynWreede.com

Instagram: jocey14941

Facebook: JocelynWreede

Made in the USA
Columbia, SC
03 July 2024